MYSTERY RIVER

A Problem-Based Ecology Unit

MYSTERY RIVER
A Problem-Based Ecology Unit

Mark A. Bohland

Prufrock Press Inc.
Waco, Texas

Access to free, downloadable student handouts for this book is available at http://www.prufrock.com/mysteryriver.

Edited by Lacy Elwood
Production Design by Marjorie Parker

ISBN-13: 978-1-59363-315-8
ISBN-10: 1-59363-315-7

Prufrock Press Inc.
P.O. Box 8813
Waco, TX 76714-8813
Phone: (800) 998-2208
Fax: (800) 240-0333
http://www.prufrock.com

Contents

Acknowledgements

I would like to acknowledge the following people, without whom this book would not exist:

- Lydia Smith, who insisted that all students could and would learn to read, and for whom failure was not an option. The inspiration in this book for students collecting mussel shells and using them to demonstrate place value, as well as the grouping and regrouping of numbers, came from a fond memory of collecting sticks behind my elementary school, during the early weeks of first grade. Thank you, Ms. Smith.

- Deborah, my wife, who read countless revisions of the manuscript, and who encourages me to take the time to think and create.

- My school administrators and supervisors who support nontraditional learning (as long as the academic content standards are learned).

- My students, who know the differences between "to," "too," and "two," which my spell checker does not, and who challenge my logic and presentation.

- The following people and organizations, who generously offered their time and resources during the early developmental stages of this book:
    - the Ohio Department of Natural Resources, Division of Wildlife;
    - the Ohio Environmental Protection Agency;
    - the Columbus Zoo and Aquarium;
    - the Ohio State University; and
    - Mr. Steve McKee and the Gorman Nature Center.

- And especially, three sixth-grade students who discovered dozens of "typos" as the original drafts of these pages were first used in their classroom, and then twice scoured the later drafts of the manuscript for this book during summer vacation. Thank you to Kristine Pfister, April Piper, and Robert Stevens.

Introduction

Why Problem-Based Learning (PBL)?

Whether teaching students who are identified as gifted or trying to meet the needs of high-ability students in a mixed-ability classroom, teachers often are confronted with the dilemma of choosing between content and process. This dilemma only has intensified as education has become more standards driven. Some teachers opt for an emphasis on acceleration—merely moving students to the next item on the curriculum map without regard to developing the student's depth of knowledge, let alone developing the student's ability to use content in a meaningful way. Others focus on activities purported to develop higher level thinking skills, but which, in too many instances, are merely fun and games with little correlation to the content standards of the curriculum.

A problem-based learning (PBL) unit is specifically designed for student-centered learning of new and meaningful content in a way that forces students to grapple with a complex and changing problem, requiring higher level thinking skills in an environment where students work both individually and collaboratively.

The *Mystery River* Problem

Indian Hill is a peaceful neighborhood on the southeast edge of the fictional town of Capitol City. No longer purely rural, but certainly not all city, Indian Hill is a neighborhood in transition. On the one hand, community traditions older than most parents and grandparents in the community are still enjoyed by families, especially by the children who attend the two neighborhood schools that have managed to survive mergers and building programs. On the other hand, students are receiving the benefits of school/business collaborations with two cutting-edge, nationally recognized companies located in the community.

An annual fall festival that alternates location between the two neighborhood schools is in its 82nd year. Each school celebrates traditions within the larger festival tradition. Of particular note is the fourth-grade Native American jewelry art project. Mussel shells collected from a stream bank that forms Hopewell Elementary's eastern property edge are used for various class activities, including the jewelry-making project.

Although the quantity of shells may have been decreasing over the last several years, it has been so slow of a decrease that no one (especially not teachers with busy schedules) has taken particular notice until now. The shells are gone!

Students are asked to serve as part of a community group investigating the situation to determine what, if anything, is wrong, and what, if anything, should be done. This open-ended assignment will draw students into a real-life drama. Every day new information emerges, widening, and sometimes narrowing the possibilities. However, there never seems to be enough information to be 100% sure of a conclusion. Students must look outside the materials provided in order to fill holes in their knowledge and data. With each new piece of information, students must ask new questions rather than jump to quick conclusions. That is something that can be particularly challenging for able students, who are accustomed to being rewarded for quick answers to closed-ended questions. Students also will prepare to present their findings to a panel of expert professionals from your community.

The Teacher's Role

Good teachers love teaching. However, teacher-led instruction isn't always best for students. In a PBL unit, teachers "teach" very little content, while students/learners "learn" both the content of the unit and the process of learning on their own. In a PBL environment, the teacher becomes a facilitator, a coach, and a guide, directing and helping students learn to learn on their own.

A facilitator may gently nudge a student or group of students away from a course of action that will ultimately waste their time (e.g., ideas such as "Maybe an giant condor came by and ate the mussels" or "Maybe acid rain from the sky is poisoning the river and killing the mussels"). Unless you teach this unit in a geographic location where giant condors are known to exist, or have recently had acid rain stories appearing in local or national media available to your students, these and other similar theories often are the result of students being conditioned to give quick answers rather than fully reading, researching, and studying the available material. I can assure you there is no mention of condor sightings, acid rain, or even factory smokestacks that seem to be malfunctioning in the material I have provided for students to study.

However, a facilitator may allow a student to follow an honestly researched theory, even though he or she knows the theory is not plausible. A student or group of students may show up for class with a stack of books from the local library. They obviously are researching outside the material provided. They may, however, have acquired information regarding marine (saltwater) mussels, rather than the freshwater mussels mentioned in this unit in their attempts to find additional research. Gentle questioning (while allowing students to learn on their own) often will see student groups quickly discovering that the information does not apply.

Facilitators often are pleasantly surprised when students or student groups research and advance a very plausible theory or solution that is not included in "the real answer." This has happened to me, causing me to reread my previous book, *Mystery Disease*, when my students discovered a very plausible scenario I hadn't realized was in the text.

Every year I use a PBL unit during the second of four grading periods in the academic year. The skills learned during the PBL unit, while working as a member of a group, are much the same as those needed when the same students participate in an independent study during the second half of the school year.

The Student's Role

The curriculum in a PBL unit is not merely "more of the same." Students not only explore the depth and breadth of content, they also use newly acquired knowledge in complex and practical ways. They process that content knowledge, make connections with prior knowledge, and evaluate various positions and alternative theories. They do this while solving problems, learning to work both as an individual and as part of a group, and making a public presentation of their theory and plan of action.

All of this learning takes place in the context of a real-world problem, which itself makes learning more meaningful and interesting to students. Teachers will find this PBL unit to be a refreshing and exciting way to facilitate learning among bright and gifted learners, as well as in mixed-ability classrooms. A PBL unit maximizes the use of limited time, allowing for both content acquisition and process skills development in a way that is both exciting and challenging for students.

Getting Started

Preview Unit

You will play the role of Mr. Stevens, a community liaison for the State Department of Streams and Wildlife. (Note: You may edit Mr. to Mrs., Miss, Ms., or Dr. as best suits your situation.) In this capacity you will have to be familiar with each day's activities, distribute information to students, and guide students' work. Make sure to familiarize yourself with the material for *all* sessions of the unit, as well as suggested Internet resources, before introducing any of the material. This will give you a feel for the flow of the unit from session to session before you begin working with students.

As you prepare to teach this unit, you will want to consider visiting the Web site for this book, http://www.prufrock.com/mysteryriver, where you will find free access to downloadable, reproducible versions of the student handouts included in this book. You can use this resource, along with the teacher's instructions in this book, to plan a successful *Mystery River* unit in your classroom.

Make Adaptations

This unit originally was used with upper elementary and middle school students in a full-day pullout program that met once a week. It could just as easily (and maybe more easily) be used in a class that meets every day. In a full-day program, one "session" was introduced in the morning and the next "session" was introduced in the afternoon. If your class meets daily, you may want to do one session per day. However, you may want to include an extra day or two between some of the later sessions to give students adequate time to prepare for presentations.

Using the Internet

The unit assumes that students have Internet access in the classroom. Although this unit is not a WebQuest, it makes extensive use of Internet resources. The unit can be used without student Internet access if you are willing to provide copies of relevant information (along with a fair number of irrelevant "red herring" pages) you have found from your own Internet searches. You also may be able to find background information, as well as free posters for your classroom, from your state's department of natural resources.

Some students may need a bit of a push in the right direction during the first session. Several relevant search terms are included on page 8.

Allocating Time

This unit is designed to be completed in 15 sessions. Sessions 1 and 2 should be combined if at all possible to increase student interest. Session 2 may need to be extended to a second class day if you do not have a large block of time with your students. Typically, you will need about 2 hours for each of the sessions. On the day of presentations, you will need about 10 minutes per group for the actual presentation, with an additional 5 minutes per group for the judges to write comments and tabulate scores. You also may plan 5–10 minutes prior to the presentations to share the PBL concept with parents and other guests who are attending the presentations. Another 10–20 minutes may be planned after the presentations for students to interact with judges and for the judges to share relevant experiences from their jobs, as well as career-planning information.

Selecting Judges

You will need three judges to evaluate the students' final presentations. People who have a background in wildlife management or nature education often make good judges. Explain how much time they will be asked to devote to the evaluations. Schedule a date for the presentations that is acceptable to all of the judges. You may want to have a backup judge in case one of the judges drops out at the last minute.

Make copies of all of the materials for each judge, and give the materials to him or her well in advance of the presentations, so he or she has plenty of time to become familiar with the problem. The judges' packets should include all parent and student handouts, as well as the Note to Judges on pages 80–81, and the Judges' Evaluation Form on page 82.

Grouping Students

Determine optimal student groupings for your class. Three to six students per group will work; four or five is ideal. Consider whether you will have groups composed of students who have demonstrated leadership in the past and additional groups composed of followers, or whether you want groups composed of a mixture of leaders and followers. Also, think about whether you want mixed-grade-level groups or single-grade-level groups. Ultimately, you want to choose groupings that will be best for your students.

Assign or have each group choose a leader. Groups also may choose a group name. Choosing an appropriate group name may be easier after the third or fourth session.

Class Session	Simulation Day	Simulation Date	Pages Used
1	N/A	N/A	10–17
2	1	Oct. 9	18–21
3	5	Oct.13	22–24
4	8	Oct. 16	25–29
5	12	Oct. 20	30–32
6	12	Oct. 20	33–35
7	12	Oct. 20	36–49
8	13	Oct. 21	50–64
9	15	Oct. 23	65–69
10	15	Oct. 23	70–73
11	18	Oct. 26	74
12	19	Oct. 27	75–76
13	20	Oct. 28	77
14	21	Oct. 29	78
15	22	Oct. 30	79–82

Figure 1. Simulated calendar

Planning the Unit

In a one-day-per-week full-day pullout program, I covered two sessions per school day for the first 7 weeks of the 8 actual weeks allocated to this unit during a 9-week grading period. See Figure 1 for a simulated calendar that can be used to help plan the unit's lessons and activities.

Standards

Problem-based learning naturally addresses standards from multiple content areas. *Mystery River* addresses standards in science, math, social studies, and language arts. A nonexhaustive list includes:

Science
- Differentiate between the life cycles of different plants and animals.
- Analyze plant and animal structures and functions needed for survival and describe the flow of energy through a system that all organisms use to survive.
- Compare changes in an organism's ecosystem/habitat that affect its survival.
- Organize and evaluate observations, measurements, and other data to formulate inferences and conclusions.
- Design a solution or product taking into account needs and constraints (e.g., cost, time, trade-offs, properties of materials, safety, and aesthetics).
- Give examples of how thinking scientifically is helpful in daily life.

Math
- Represent and analyze patterns, rules, and functions with words, tables, graphs, and simple variable expressions.
- Generalize patterns by describing in words how to find the next term.
- Recognize and explain when numerical patterns are linear or nonlinear progressions (e.g., 1, 3, 5, 7 . . . is linear and 1, 3, 4, 8, 16 . . . is nonlinear).

Social Studies
- Compare multiple viewpoints and frames of reference related to important events in world history.
- Establish guidelines, rules, and timelines for group work.
- Reflect on the performance of a classroom group in which one has participated including the contribution of each member in reaching group goals.
- Give an oral presentation that includes citation of sources.
- Identify ways to manage conflict within a group.

Language Arts
- Identify and understand organizational patterns (e.g., cause-effect, problem-solution) and techniques, including repetition of ideas and word choice, that authors use to accomplish their purpose.
- Critique the treatment, scope, and organization of ideas from multiple sources on the same topic.
- Produce presentations that:
  o demonstrate an understanding of the topic and present events or ideas in a logical sequence;

- support the controlling idea or thesis with well-chosen and relevant facts, details, examples, quotations, statistics, and stories;
- include an effective introduction and conclusion and use a consistent organizational structure (e.g., cause-effect, compare-contrast, problem-solution);
- use appropriate visual materials (e.g., diagrams, charts, illustrations) and available technology to enhance presentation; and
- draw from multiple sources and identify sources used.

Assessment

Problem-based learning presupposes authentic assessment. I utilize judges who are professionals in the area of the problem students are studying to evaluate student presentations. I only evaluate students' individual participation/effort and group cooperation/participation.

In my classes, students are assessed three times. The judges assess students' collection and observation of data and evidence, their logical interpretation of that information, their ability to create a plausible solution to the perceived problem, and their presentation of that solution. They do this using the Judges Evaluation Form on page 82. I (as facilitator) assess, and students self-assess, both content acquisition and process skills using the Learner/Facilitator Evaluation Form on pages 85–86.

Students should know ahead of time how they will be assessed. Exactly when to do that may different for each group of students, but I generally shares both the Judge's Evaluation Form and the Learner/Facilitator Evaluation Form with students somewhere between the fourth and sixth sessions. I wait until the students are comfortable with this new learning process, so as to not burden them with the thought of evaluation prior to having a sense of what is going on.

Some facilitators also may find they are requested/required to assess content acquisition with an outmoded pencil-and-paper test. If that is the case, I suggest inviting an administrator to the presentations to determine whether he or she will accept the presentation as a valid alternative assessment. If not, you may at least be permitted to use the presentations as a factor (e.g., extra credit, single question or essay substitution) in determining the students' final grades. In addition, there is an answer key located at the back of this book to help you with a few of the items that do have answers.

Other Resources

As you work through the sessions in this book, you may desire additional information on a variety of topics. The following resources will help you garner that information.

Problem-Based Learning

http://www.udel.edu/pbl
http://www.mcli.dist.maricopa.edu/pbl/info.html
http://www.pbli.org

Inquiry-Based Learning

http://www.thirteen.org/edonline/concept2class/inquiry/index_sub1.html

Group/Team Building Activities

http://www.irondale.org/gguide/gb.htm
http://www.wavemakers.ca
http://www.wilderdom.com/teambuilding

Group Decision-Making Skills

http://www.foundationcoalition.org/home/keycomponents/teams/
   decision1.html
http://www.foundationcoalition.org/home/keycomponents/teams/
   decision2.html
http://www.foundationcoalition.org/home/keycomponents/teams/
   decision3.html

Public Speaking Skills

http://www.wikihow.com/Do-a-Presentation-in-Class

Potential Internet Search Terms to Aid in Finding Information on the Problem

Have your students open a search engine. Then, they should type in "freshwater mussels" and any of the following terms:

- endangered
- stream water quality
- siltation
- extinction
- indicator species
- runoff
- pollution
- life cycle
- reproduction

Free Software

http://www.abisource.com

Very much like Microsoft Word, this is great for students who do not have Microsoft Word at home. It can save with .doc extension.

http://www.coolfreesoftware.com

Create your own word search puzzles.

http://www.sunrisesunset.com

Good for science class or other applications at school. Calculates sunrise and sunset (twilight, total daylight, sun overhead, etc.) for any location in the world—just enter your school's latitude and longitude.

Free Trial Software

http://www.crosswordkit.com

Create your own crossword puzzles with this 30-day full capability trial. At the end of the trial period, the software is only $25.

http://www.digitalphotoslideshow.com

More than just slideshows from your pictures, this site is a very good image resizer and Web page creator.

This site is great for a school's open house or parents' night to display student work. Includes a 60-day full capability trial. At the end of the trial period, the software is only $20.

Session 1

Session 1 is conducted before the simulation begins.

Materials: Student Handout A, Parent Handout A, Parent Handout B on pages 12–17

Session Goals:
1. Let students know how they will be evaluated in this unit using the Judges Evaluation Form (see p. 82). Tell students the judges will be evaluating them on what they know, their logical interpretation of what they know, and their ability to present what they know to others in an informative and persuasive way.
2. Let students know that the unique contributions of each team member will affect the success of the team as a whole.
3. Help students understand the definition of the word *problem*. Help students understand the difference between a problem like "What is the average height of the students in you class?" and a real-world problem like those mentioned in the student and parent handouts for this session.
4. Inform parents of what their children will be doing for the rest of this unit, and make them aware of the public group presentations at the end of the unit.

Procedures:
1. Begin by asking students:
    a. how they think problems on school tests differ from problems in adult life,
    b. how adults are judged or graded in their job performance,
    c. what sort of steps they use to work through problems outside of school,
    d. what makes a good team, and
    e. what makes a good team member.
2. Discuss the handouts (including the parent handouts) and encourage students to discuss them with their parents.
3. Assign or allow students to chose groups.

What You'll See: Students will become excited about the prospect of working in groups. They will become excited about the idea of a "fuzzy" problem with the possibility of more than one right answer.

What Could Go Wrong:
- PBL requires considerable frontloading for students who have never learned this way. The first session could get a bit long and tedious, and a break with a fun activity is helpful about halfway through.

- Students may agree that building a team is different from just choosing friends, but unless the "choosers" are mature and can pick team members based on a variety of ability traits, it might be better for the teacher to assign teams.

Fuzzy Challenge Procedures

A "Fuzzy Challenge" is called *fuzzy* because what you need to do to succeed in the assignment is not clear at the start of the assignment. Everything seems a little bit fuzzy.

Fuzzy Challenge assignments are very much like real-life situations. Often, owners, directors, managers, employees, and employee teams in businesses and organization are presented with a task—a challenge—that needs to be completed, but they don't currently have the necessary information, resources, or plan to successfully complete the assignment.

The goal of their assignment may be to "increase sales," "find a cure," "make the client happy," or "design a new program to meet a specific need." However, they may not know exactly what steps must be taken to accomplish the goal.

Before the assignment can be completed, the people working on it must discover what they need to know. To be successful, they must design a plan to accomplish the task, and finally, they must implement their plan. There may be several different, but acceptable, ways of accomplishing the goal.

It also is quite possible that there are other individuals or teams working on the same project without their knowledge. Coming up with a better solution to the assignment than other individuals or groups may mean a pay raise, a promotion, or even the success or failure of their company or organization. It also is quite possible that situations and needs can change while they are solving the problem. A new law may be passed that will force them to change something they wanted to do.

Here are some basic steps used to successfully complete a Fuzzy Challenge:

1. Define
    a. Restate the assignment in specific terms.
    b. List areas of inadequate knowledge.
    c. Ask yourself where you can acquire the necessary knowledge.
2. Design
    a. Determine what needs to be done.
    b. Determine how it will be done.
    c. Determine who will do what parts.
3. Do
    a. Do it.
4. Determine
    a. Potential for success.
    b. Repeat steps 1–3 in areas of weakness.
5. Debrief
    a. Analyze the success of the project.

A Note to Parents

Dear Parents,

We are about to begin a new problem-based learning (PBL) unit of study. This is a group-learning activity designed to challenge your students on several levels. Because this may be a very different learning experience from what your child has experienced before, I should share a few observations and guidelines with you.

1. Your student will need to learn much of what he or she needs to know on his or her *own* or in conjunction with his or her team members.
2. Many students will want to share their successes with their parents.
3. Many students will want to try to get "answers" and/or excessive help from parents.

Please be willing to listen to your student and to offer help in the form of allowing him or her Internet access, or taking him or her to the library or other research location that *he or she* suggests. However, please do not offer your own insights or information even when asked. If your child asks a question about the content/topic of this PBL unit, you may want to consider answering with, "What do you think?"

If he or she wants your opinion regarding a theory or possible course of action, you may want to consider answering with, "That's an interesting idea. Why do you say that?"

One of the fundamental concepts of PBL is that students can learn to be learners—that is, they can learn to learn on their own, without the overriding presence of a teacher. The teacher then becomes a facilitator, whose task it is to help the student learn to learn, rather than to teach the specific content of the problem.

Thank you in advance for your cooperation and help during this learning experience. We'll look forward to seeing you on the day of the group presentations.

Sincerely,

Teacher's Name

A Parent's Introduction to Problem-Based Learning

Dear Parents,

As we begin a new unit, I think it would be a good idea to let you know what sort of challenge your student will be facing. For some students, this will be the most exciting and challenging thing they have ever done in school. For others it may seem like the most overwhelming and challenging thing they have ever done. In either case, it will be challenging.

It will not be challenging because of the actual difficulty of the assignment, but because they may have never participated in this type of learning exercise before. We will be engaging in a problem-based learning unit that will offer students the opportunity to learn about public stream water quality, endangered species, governmental problem solving, social science and systems, public speaking, and much more.

Please ask to see all of the materials I have given your student for his or her Fuzzy Challenge. We are calling this unit a Fuzzy Challenge, simply because that seems to describe what students are doing better than problem-based learning. However, the terms are interchangeable.

So, what is Problem-Based Learning (PBL) anyway? Here is the way it was explained to the students:

Fuzzy Challenges are designed to help students learn new information in a way that is very similar to real-world, adult situations. Suppose we have a flooded baseball field. I could give several "assignments" to my ball field committee:

1. Dig a ditch from the field to the creek, drain the field, order sand and dirt from a named local supplier, and repair the ball field, using park department employees and equipment.
2. Get the field in shape to play ball next week.
3. Get the field ready for our Fourth of July picnic.

Each assignment is less specific and fuzzier than the one before it.

1. The committee knows exactly what is expected.
2. The committee knows the goal, but they are free to accomplish it as they see fit.
3. The committee knows that something needs to be accomplished, but at this point they are not even sure what that is. (Do we get the field into playing condition for baseball, or make sure it stays flooded and stock it with trout for a children's fishing contest?)

In PBL, much of the assignment is stated in fuzzy terms. The students first must restate the problem to make sure they are headed in the right direction. (There is no sense solving the wrong problem.) They must then ask themselves what knowledge or skills are necessary to solve the problem and which of those they currently lack.

This is where some students will want to give up. In PBL they will *not* be spoon-fed.

If (in the previous example) *they* determine that the committee chairman wants a fishing derby, they will *not* be told to call Fender's Fish Company in Danville, OH, find out the cost of a dozen trout, and then determine the total cost of 240 trout, if the company gives a 5% discount on purchases of 200 or more fish.

That would be no more than a simple word problem, combined with an exercise in telephone etiquette. Problem-based learning is much more realistic than that.

In a PBL unit, they might be asked to present a report to the committee chairman, detailing their plans for utilizing the flooded ball field for a children's fishing derby, during the Fourth of July weekend.

Students would be divided into work teams, and would present their competing plans on the final day of the unit. This simulates competing project teams in a large corporation. Students may ask the committee chairman (their teacher) relevant questions, which he may or may not answer.

Because the teacher wants all groups working on the same problem, he would answer questions such as: How many children do we expect? (150 children.) Will we provide fishing gear, or do participants bring their own? (We will provide identical fishing poles for each child.) Are parents allowed to fish too? (No.) Will the field stay flooded or do we have to keep it flooded? (It will stay flooded.) Do we need a permit or insurance? (Permit: Not sure, check with the game warden. Insurance: No, we already have it.)

Because the teacher wants students to be creative, independent learners, he will *not* answer questions like: What kind of fish works best for a children's fishing derby? Where do I find a fish farm? How will they be shipped to our field? What are the shipping costs? How do we keep them alive? What kind of fishing poles should we get? How much do fishing poles cost? Where should we buy them? Who is the game warden? What is our budget? What hours will we be open?

This year's Fuzzy Challenge, "Mystery River," is outlined in the information in your student's folder. Please encourage your student to have fun with this project. Ask him or her to share the unit information with you, and to explain to you, what he or she *doesn't* know but *needs to know* to complete the assignment.

As the students work through this "what-do-I-need-to-know-but-don't-know" phase, and then find the information they need to know to complete the assignment, *this is where the real self-directed learning takes place.* Please don't let your student give up or become overwhelmed at this critical point. This is where our students will learn (in addition to specific content) the skills that will stand them in good stead as they prepare to enter young adulthood.

When our students have learned how to identify their own areas of inadequate knowledge, how to acquire that knowledge on their own, and how to then apply that knowledge to the problem at hand, they will have gained a skill that will be invaluable to them, regardless of their chosen career or vocation.

This is the real goal of this unit. Anything else they learn about stream quality and endangered species is a bonus.

This unit will require limited out-of-class work, but it should be fun. Please allow your student to use the phone, the computer, or the public library as necessary. (Encourage the use of toll-free numbers.) Previous Fuzzy Challenge groups have found a small parent-sponsored field trip to be invaluable.

Although we have couched this problem-based learning unit in science and social studies terms, if your student really gets stuck or disheartened, encourage him or her to think of the unit as a mystery puzzle. In fact, after successfully completing this unit, these students should be able to assist you in any number of real-world problems.

Problem-based learning helps meet the needs of many of our students who need a more authentic learning environment, and it also addresses many of the higher level learning standards included in most state academic content standards. Although not an exhaustive list, we will address the following standards:

- Differentiate between the life cycles of different plants and animals.
- Analyze plant and animal structures and functions needed for survival and describe the flow of energy through a system that all organisms use to survive.
- Compare changes in an organism's ecosystem/habitat that affect its survival.
- Organize and evaluate observations, measurements, and other data to formulate inferences and conclusions.
- Design a solution or product taking into account needs and constraints (e.g., cost, time, trade-offs, properties of materials, safety, and aesthetics).
- Give examples of how thinking scientifically is helpful in daily life.

I have included Web site addresses below for more information on the concept of PBL, which detail the theory behind the method, as well as its use in medical schools and other institutions of higher learning:

- http://www.udel.edu/pbl
- http://www.mcli.dist.maricopa.edu/pbl/info.html
- http://www.pbli.org

As usual, I am available to speak with you individually regarding this unit or your child's personal needs and progress. I consider it a privilege to work with your child.

Sincerely,

Teacher's Name

Session 2

Materials: Student Handout 1, on pages 20–21; Internet access for students

Session Goals:

1. Introduce Internet search techniques, Web site evaluation, and Internet safety.
2. Encourage students to utilize information sources other than the Internet.
3. Introduce the problem.

Procedures:

1. Have students sit with their group members. Begin by:
   a. discussing school Internet-use policies,
   b. asking students how they find information on the Internet,
   c. emphasizing the use of approved search engine sites,
   d. asking students to share other ways of finding information, and
   e. stressing that you will not be giving them everything they need to know to solve their problem (if indeed there is a problem), and that they must take responsibility for their own learning from a variety of sources.
2. Have the students take turns reading Student Handout 1 aloud. As the last student finishes, *remain silent*.
3. Wait until a student asks a question—usually something like, "What do you want us to do? Your answer to this question (and most other questions asked during this unit) should take the form of, "What do you think would be a good thing to do now?" Another student may ask, "Can we go to the library," or "Can we get online?" Your response should be, "Do you think that would be a good idea?" When students finally say, "Yes," try to simply say something like, "Good," "Cool," or "I'm glad to see you can think that through." Avoid giving permission or otherwise acting as though they are not responsible for their own decisions and actions.

What You'll See: Students may become convinced that the first piece of data or information they discover *must* be the right answer. They may assume that the problem can be solved in 20 minutes rather than 8–10 weeks. This is a result of the way they have been expected to respond to questions in the past. Encourage them to view new information as a starting point for yet another new question.

What Could Go Wrong:

- If students do not have Internet access, the teacher may create a large quantity of printouts from Web pages. Care should be taken to include printouts with interesting but irrelevant materials.
- Students may get excited about things they find on the Internet that are interesting, but are irrelevant to their problem.

Mystery River

The first weeks of school are always fun and exciting for the students of Hopewell Elementary School. Even though Capitol City is the largest city in the state, the students at Hopewell Elementary often imagine they live far away from the city in a different time and place. That is easy for them to do. Their school is on the southern edge of the city, and is surrounded on three sides by Hopewell Park, one of the city's 12 metro parks. Across the road from the school is a neighborhood of large homes. Behind the school flows the Shawnee River. Many young students at Hopewell Elementary have looked across the river and imagined themselves to be one of the Native Americans who lived along this river centuries ago.

When the grandparents of Hopewell Elementary School students were children, the area around the school was considered to be "way out in the country." Some of those grandparents now live in the new retirement center just south of Hopewell Park. As the city grew and incorporated more and more land, eventually this area also became part of Capitol City. That is when the land around the school became Hopewell Park, Capitol City's largest metro park. Hopewell Park is home to many kinds of wildlife not seen in other areas of the city.

The Shawnee River flows to the south through Hopewell Park. At one point the river forms the eastern edge of Hopewell Elementary School's property. Students whose rooms are on the east side of the building often see a deer or two drinking from the river early in the morning. Mrs. Peterson keeps several sets of binoculars near the window for her students to use when they see something special near the river. Each year Mrs. Peterson has her fifth-grade students make a chart of what they see near the river.

Most of the large industrial companies are located across the city on the northwest side of town. There are a few midsize companies here on the southeast side of town, but even they have buildings and landscaping that help them blend in to the rest of the community. Many of the students at Hopewell Elementary have parents who work at Compu-Systems and BioTech, two of Capitol City's newer companies in this part of town.

One of the highlights of early autumn is the annual Adena/Hopewell School Festival. Adena Elementary School is another of Capitol City School's elementary schools, and is located about 2 miles north of Hopewell Elementary. The two "sister schools" have held their combined festival for as many years as anyone can remember. On odd numbered years, the festival is held at Adena Elementary, and on even numbered years it is held at Hopewell Elementary.

Mrs. Whitehead is the art teacher at Hopewell Elementary School. Every year she and Miss Smith (a first-grade teacher) take the first graders to the east edge of the school property to collect clam shells like the Native Americans used to do. The shells from several varieties of freshwater mussels are left scattered along the back of the school property by muskrats and an occasional otter, for which the mussels are a major food source. Miss Smith uses the small shells to help students learn about grouping numbers and place value. She also shares a few shells with another class that creates a display depicting the local food web. Mrs. Whitehead uses the largest number of shells for her fourth-grade art classes.

In Mrs. Whitehead's art class, students create jewelry that looks like the authentic Native American shell jewelry that can be seen in a local museum. Then they get to wear and display their jewelry at the Adena/Hopewell School Festival. Students look forward to the fourth-grade jewelry project for several years.

In previous years, a long undisturbed summer, the animals along the river have left enough shells on the bank of the river at the back of the school property, for everyone in the fourth grade to make two or three nice pieces of jewelry. This year, however, when the first graders went out to collect shells, they only found three shells. The teachers thought that something must be terribly wrong. Mrs. Whitehead immediately called her friend at the State Department of Streams and Wildlife (DSW) in Capitol City.

When questioned, Mrs. Whitehead recalled that over the last several years, there seemed to be somewhat fewer shells than before, but she didn't think much of it. Now, she recalls that last year most of the fourth graders only made one piece of jewelry, but still she had been so busy with getting ready for the festival, she completely forgot about it until now.

Word of the disappearing clam shells spread quickly through the community, especially after a reporter from a community newspaper attended the school festival and reported the disappointment among fourth graders who had to make their jewelry out of paper and plastic this year. Now, community leaders throughout the city are becoming concerned. People are wondering whether this is a normal cyclical phenomenon or whether the mussels are gone forever. Are the mussels experiencing temporarily low populations, or have they become extinct?

You have been asked to be on a committee to investigate the problem. Your job is to determine what, if anything, is wrong, and what, if anything, needs to be done and can be done. Your committee is to make its report and recommendations, if any, to the State Department of Streams and Wildlife, 3 weeks from today.

I will serve as the liaison between your group and the DSW between now and the time of your presentation. You may contact me if you have any questions.

a Stevens

Mr. Stevens
DSW Community Liaison
October 9

Materials: Student Handouts 2 and 3 on pages 23–24; Internet access for students

Session Goals:

1. Help students avoid fatal lines of research or reasoning.
2. Encourage students to begin to utilize separate sources of data to develop a theory or come to a conclusion.
3. Encourage students to express understanding in multiple ways and to communicate that understanding in a coherent paragraph of complete sentences.

Procedures:

1. Have students sit with their group members.
2. Begin by giving students Student Handout 2
3. Have someone read it aloud and remain silent.
4. If students have not developed a sense of responsibility and ownership for their own learning, they again may ask questions regarding what they are supposed to do next. Respond as before, asking them what they think would be good, helpful, or necessary to do now, or what would be an appropriate, wise, or efficient use of their time. *One of your main unit goals is to help develop self-learners.*
5. About halfway through the session, pass out Student Handout 3. Have students work individually for about 5–10 minutes, and then have them work together to come up with one answer that is acceptable to the whole group.

What You'll See: Students may become excited and encouraged as they discover new information. However, if some of the groups tend to have more natural leaders than natural followers, you may begin to see the first signs of dissention or conflict within the group. *Another unit goal is to help develop students who can work effectively in groups.*

What Could Go Wrong:

- The stark minimalism of Student Handout 2 may come as a shock to students who are used to being spoon-fed factoids for later regurgitation on a so-called test. Although some learners will be delighted at the freedom implied by such a handout, others may become frustrated that you are "not teaching us anything," or that "this is too hard."
- Students may be used to answering questions in a word or two, and may find it difficult to express understanding in a coherent paragraph. You may need to model quality sentence and paragraph forms for technical or expository writing.

Common Student Information as of the Beginning of Session 3

The following information was given to one or more groups during Session 1:

1. Zebra mussels are not a concern in this river system.

2. Hopewell Elementary School is a small school with only two classes in grades kindergarten through six.

3. The mean (average) number of students in each classroom is 25 students.

4. In the past, fourth-grade students generally put three or five shells on each necklace they made.

Student Handout 3

Using the information in Items 2, 3, and 4 in Student Handout 2, and information in Student Handout 1, determine the minimum number of shells collected and used for art classes before mussel populations began to decline. Show your work and explain your answer, using complete sentences. This question requires an extended response. After showing your work, please explain your answer with a well-constructed paragraph of at least five sentences.

Show your work here:

Explain your work on the lines below.

_____

_____

_____

_____

_____

_____

_____

_____

Session 4

Materials: Student Handouts 4 and 5, on pages 26–29; Internet access for students

Session Goals:
1. Help students understand that while they are obtaining additional information, more is yet to come. Theories need to be tentative and evolving.
2. Encourage students to continue utilizing various sources of information as they investigate their problem.

Procedures:
1. Have students sit with their group members.
2. Begin by giving students Student Handout 4. Feel free to modify this handout to reflect questions being asked. If students/learners have not yet begun asking for information mentioned in this handout, you may want to spend the early part of this session having groups make lists of "What I Know" and "What I Want To Know."
3. Have someone read the handout aloud and remain silent.
4. By now, students should be catching on to the fact that they are now free to learn. Otherwise, they again may ask questions regarding what they are supposed to do next. Respond as before, asking them what they think would be good, helpful, or necessary to do now, or what would be an appropriate, wise, or efficient use of their time. *Continue to emphasize the value/necessity of becoming a self-learner.*
5. About halfway through the session, pass out Student Handout 5. Ask groups quietly and individually what sources of information they have discovered *other than* the Internet.

What You'll See: Students may view the newspaper as irrelevant, especially because mussels are not mentioned. The newspaper is something you'll need to force students to return to in later sessions, as they uncover new information that can be connected with the newspaper stories to create meaning.

What Could Go Wrong:
- Students may become lethargic—assuming that by now they must surely know everything there is to know. They also may become dismissive of a group member whose ideas, understandings, and research do not conform to the group norm.

MEMO:
Date: October 16
From: Allen Stevens
To: The Shawnee River Mussel Investigation Committee
Re: Weekly Update

Thank you for volunteering to serve on the Shawnee River Mussel Investigation Committee. Your help may be just what we need to solve the mysterious disappearance of the mussels in the Shawnee River.

I have received requests from several of you, and I will do my best to get the information you requested by next week. I also will get a fairly detailed map of the area from the County Engineer.

I can tell you now that there are no dams or dam-like structures anywhere within 60 miles of Capital City. We have people doing stream water quality checks, but I do not know whether we will be able to get any chemical analysis of the water prior to your presentation 2 ½ weeks from now.

Per your request I have contacted Mrs. Peterson at Hopewell Elementary School. She has saved the wildlife sighting charts made by her students during the past 10 years. She has most of them in storage at her home, but she will get them to me as soon as possible. I will make copies of the charts and get them to you right away. Mrs. Peterson told me that her students have seen deer drinking from the stream, once or twice so far this year. One of her students claims to have seen an otter with a fish in its mouth, but none of the other students can confirm the sighting.

Thank you again for your help. I'll look forward to talking with you soon.

You may contact me if you have any questions.

a Stevens

Mr. Stevens
DSW Community Liaison

INDIAN HILL WHISPERS

Your Weekly Neighborhood Voice

Adena second-grade student Bobby Jones meets with his new adopted grandmother Adelle Cunningham at Adena Nursing Home.

Special Interest Articles:
- Students Adopt Grandparents
- Record Corn Crop Expected by Shawnee County Farmers
- Local Businesses Donate to Schools
- Annual Adena-Hopewell Festival a Success
- Area Spared in Spring Floods

STUDENT HANDOUT 5

Students Adopt Grandparents

Adena and Hopewell Elementary second-grade students have new grandparents, at least for a year. Once again, the students at two Indian Hill area elementary schools have been matched with residents of the local nursing home and retirement center.

School counselor Susan Binshaw said the school's adopt-a-grandparent program is special for both grandparents and students.

"Many of the residents at the nursing home and retirement center are very lonely, and many of our students either don't have grandparents or their grandparents live far away. It's a good match for everyone."

Binshaw started the adoption program 19 years ago during her first year as the school counselor. Since that time, second-grade students have been matched with a resident at Adena Nursing Home or Hopewell Retirement Center. The adopted grandparents and grandchildren meet during once-a-month walking field trips. The highlight of the year is the ice cream social at the end of May.

Although residents get new grandchildren each September, some children maintain contact with their grandparent for many years.

Record County Corn Crop Expected

While Capitol City has experienced rapid growth to the north and west, here at the southeast edge of the city and in the surrounding Shawnee County, much of our land has managed to remain in the hands of family farmers. This year, much of that land has been planted in corn.

Charles Lancer has farmed along the Shawnee River for more than 40 years.

"A lot has changed since my great-grandfather farmed this land," said Lancer. "When I was a boy he told me about plowing with a team of mules. Now I've got a computer up in the air-conditioned cab of my tractor."

Lancer's farm yielded more than 150 bushels of corn per acre last year, and he expects to do even better this year. With the price of corn as high as it is expected to be this

year, Lancer and other farmers have put every available acre into corn production.

"We have to rotate what we plant in a field each year to keep the ground healthy, but this year I planted ground that hadn't had anything in it for several years, and I rented as much land as I could for corn," he said.

Lancer and other area farmers are benefiting from the increased demand for ethanol-blended gasoline. A smaller,

but growing, factor is the number of homeowners who burn corn (a cost-effective, annually renewable bio-mass product) to heat their homes.

Farmers generally see lower prices for their corn in years of record harvest. However, for the last 3 years, the new demands for corn and corn byproducts have outpaced even the record yields and prices have risen alongside increased production.

Local Businesses Donate to Schools

Three local companies have each renewed their commitment to the education of local students. Mall Mart, Compu-Systems, and BioTech have announced donations to Capitol City schools again this year.

Mall Mart, one of the nation's largest retailers, has given a $750 grant to each Capitol City School System elementary school, a $1,000 grant to each middle school,

and a $1,500 grant to each high school.

Melvin Hammond, the district manager for Mall Mart presented the grants to the school superintendent at last Thursday's board meeting. Hammond told the Capitol City School Board, "Mall Mart is committed to the education of our nation's students, and we are happy to express that commitment with these grants."

Two smaller Capitol City-based companies joined Mall Mart in making financial contributions to one or more of the district's schools. BioTech, a leader in research and development of new medicines, is providing new first aid kits to all elementary students in the city, and Compu-Systems will work with teachers at Adena and Hopewell Elementary Schools to develop a new reading software program for young children.

Annual Adena–Hopewell Festival a Success

The annual Adena–Hopewell Elementary Schools Festival was a success once again this year. This is the 83rd annual heritage festival put on by the two schools.

The festival was held this year at the Hopewell Elementary School. Students, parents, grandparents, and "adopted" grandparents from the Butler Nursing Home and Shawnee Retirement Center, spent the afternoon playing age-old games that many of the grandparents learned from their parents and grandparents.

Mr. David Southwell, a lifetime resident of Shawnee County, entertained much of the crowd with historical stories and tall tales from the earliest days of the county,

when settlers and Native Americans lived close to one another in an uneasy truce.

One disappointment was the absence of the annual Hopewell School fourth-grade shell jewelry display.

The curious disappearance of the usually common mussel shells along the banks of the Shawnee River forced the students to create their jewelry from plastic and construction paper.

Area Spared During Spring Floods

The final damage reports from last spring's heavy rains and floods are in, and local residents can count their blessings. While many residents had to put up with some water in their basements, and one or two low-lying roads were flooded for several hours, Capitol City was spared any major damage. Residents 100 miles south of Capitol City were not so lucky.

An early snow melt and heavy rains caused local streams and rivers to crest just below their banks, but the Great Pontiac River crested at 3 feet over flood stage in Louistown, where many residents saw their homes washed away.

Locally, Boy Scout Troop 127 volunteered to help remove mud-encrusted debris from Crawford Creek. The debris was then hauled to the county landfill.

STUDENT HANDOUT 5

Session 5

Materials: Student Handouts 6 and 7, on pages 31–32; Internet access for students

Session Goals:
1. Continue to help students understand that while they are obtaining additional information, more is yet to come. Theories need to be tentative and evolving.
2. Encourage students to continue utilizing various sources of information as they investigate their problem. Make students aware that if they utilize only one source (e.g., the Internet) of information, then they will be seeing almost exactly what every other group is seeing. It then will become difficult for them to convince the judges that their understanding of the problem (if there is one) and their solution to it, is any better than any other team's understanding and solution.
3. Encourage students to continue to view information and data not so much as "answers," but rather, as that which generates more questions.

Procedures:
1. Give students Student Handout 6 to add to their growing stack of information. Students can use this handout on their own time as they further develop their solution to the problem.
2. Have students sit with their group members.
3. Begin by giving students Student Handout 7.
4. Pose a question that is relevant to your students—something like, "Should our school eliminate pizza from the lunch menu?"
5. Offer one piece of information or data relating to the question.
6. Have individuals place the question at the top of the handout and the information or data above the "What I Know" arrow.
7. They should then complete the knowledge tree. Remain silent while they do so.
8. Have the entire class share their knowledge trees and discuss their results.

What You'll See: You should begin to see students making connections among the data and information they have collected. Some enterprising groups or individuals may have convinced parents to take them on their own out-of-school mini-field trip.

What Could Go Wrong:
- Other students may have become overreliant on one source of information.

MEMO:
Date: October 20
From: Allen Stevens
To: The Shawnee River Mussel Investigation Committee
Re: Midweek Update

Thank you again for all of your help. Your hard work is a positive example to everyone in this community.

The County Engineer contacted me early this morning. He has assured me that we will receive the maps you requested later today.

Mrs. Peterson told me that yesterday three of her students were using the classroom binoculars to watch a doe and two fawns drinking at the river. While watching the deer, all three students saw a pair of otters playing along the bank of the Shawnee River.

The students were curious about the police cars they saw parked at the school when they arrived yesterday. Teachers told students that police officers were helping the Department of Streams and Wildlife rangers investigate the disappearance of mussels in the river. What teachers did not tell students was that when the custodian and principal arrived at school earlier in the morning, they found a large deer laying near the back of the school yard. It had been shot and killed, and its antlers had been removed. The legal hunting season for deer does not begin for several weeks, and hunting is not even allowed within the Capitol City limits.

Mrs. Peterson apologized for not having the wildlife charts ready today. She has been very busy unpacking all of the wonderful supplies that were given to the school by BioTech. In addition to the donations made to all of the other Capitol City elementary schools, BioTech has made special donations to the two Indian Hills neighborhood schools. Every student at Adena and Hopewell Elementary Schools will receive a first aid kit designed for their home and one for their parents' car. Each classroom also will get an age-appropriate "Discover Chemistry" set. Mrs. Peterson said she is almost finished unpacking all of the supplies, and she promised to get the wildlife charts to me by tomorrow. I'll make copies of them and get a copy to you as soon as possible.

Thank you again for your help. I'll look forward to talking with you soon.

You may contact me if you have any questions.

A. Stevens

Mr. Stevens
DSW Community Liaison

STUDENT HANDOUT 6

Name: _____   Date: _____

Knowledge Tree

My Question Is: _____

Which makes me wonder . . . .

Is it possible that . . . .

I wish I knew if . . . .

What I want to know . . . .

Which makes me wonder . . . .

What I know . . . .
(first piece of related
information or data)

© Prufrock Press Inc. • *Mystery River*

Session 6

Materials: Student Handout 8, on pages 34–35; Internet access for students during the second half of the session (optional)

Session Goal:

1. Help students to understand that information or data that was previously deemed irrelevant may indeed have value in light of new material.

Procedures:

1. Have students sit with their group members.
2. Begin by giving students Student Handout 8. Remain silent.

What You'll See: Some groups may grasp the significance of older information and data as they are exposed to this new information. However, other groups may merely glance at the newspaper and immediately ask, "Can we get on the Internet now?" Others who have at least learned that they are permitted to choose what they will do with their time may simply go to the computers and get online. In a sense this is good, because they are beginning to act like self-learners. Nevertheless, as a facilitator you may have to guide (sometimes insist) students to an understanding that today, time could be better spent reviewing and making connections about the data and information they already possess. During the second half of the session you may want to allow Internet access, but with the warning that they must be finding information elsewhere, and that Internet research will end two sessions from now.

What Could Go Wrong:

- Some students may be experiencing a level of frustration that is impeding progress. (In my experience, it happened at Session 8.) If that is the case, you may want to devote part of the class to lateral thinking techniques or activities. If you do not have activities of your own, you may want to use Handouts 23 and 24 (pp. 52–53) here, instead of during Session 8.

Capitol City Dispatch

—October 20, Issue 23

Legislature Debates Energy

The state legislature has begun debate on a comprehensive energy bill that could affect citizens of this state for the next hundred years. The new set of laws, if passed and signed by the governor, would affect everything from how the state heats its buildings to what kind of gasoline each of us will put in our car.

As written, the State Energy Independence Bill would require the state energy department to establish "a clear set of achievable, affordable and enforceable" guidelines that would be phased in over the next 5 years. The goal of the guidelines would be to reduce the state's dependence on foreign energy sources by 60% by the year 2030.

The ambitious law would require state-owned buildings

to be converted to alternative energy sources for at least 60% of the energy required for heating and cooling those buildings.

Under the proposed law, homeowners would receive a credit on their state income tax for the installation of approved home heating or cooling systems that

operate on alternative energy sources. Geothermal- and wind-powered systems would be included, and new technologies could be approved as they become available. A special credit would be given for people using annually renewable biomass products to heat their homes or to heat water.

BioTech Leads Nation in Free Drugs

BioTech Pharmaceuticals has just become the nation's leader in providing free and low-cost generic drugs to people with special needs. By teaming up with Mall Mart, Ball Green, Grin Pixie, and a dozen or so pharmacies operated by national chain grocery stores, Capitol City's fastest growing company has managed to

provide more drugs to the poor than any other drug manufacturer in the nation.

BioTech president Charles Wentworth reacted to the news. "We're just pleased to be able to help where we can. Since the FDA approved Calmmax, our sales have tripled, stock prices are up, and it looks like we will finally

be making a profit 2 years in a row. Now, it is time for us to celebrate by giving back to the community."

In addition to the recently approved wonder drug for treating mood swings and depression, BioTech also manufactures dozens of commonly used generic *continued on next page*

BioTech, from front page

drugs. "Here at BioTech, we manufacture medicines that are taken by millions of people every day," Wentworth said.

When asked about the company's free drug program, Wentworth said, "I see the need every day. My mother is a resident at Butler Nursing Home, and although she can afford her medicine, many of the residents cannot. By providing low- and no-cost medicine, we can help people throughout the world have a better life."

Locally, Dr. Deborah Whitehead, director of patient care at Butler Nursing Home, said the donations from BioTech have been wonderful, but sometimes they are even more than the nursing home can use.

"It seems a shame to waste medicine, but once it reaches its expiration date, we just have to get rid of it the best way we can," she said.

Once a month, most nursing homes and retirement centers have a medicine check-and-flush day to dispose of old drugs.

Poachers Arrested

State wildlife officers arrested seven men and seized thousands of dollars worth of plant and animal parts, as well as guns, traps, computers, cash, and other evidence. One Department of State Wildlife (DSW) officer called this the biggest bust in recent history.

Seized material included deer antlers, fur pelts, and plant parts that would have been legal if collected by licensed hunters during an open hunting or gathering season. Officers also seized plant and animal parts from protected species.

"It's all about the money," said the DSW officer, who works undercover. "There is a huge market both here and overseas for certain plant and animal parts. The poachers hurt everyone in the state. In some cases, it is a matter of stealing what would have been someone else's trophy deer. Other times, poachers destroy endangered species and, over time, actually can contribute to a species' extinction.

"There is no telling where poached materials may end up. Antlers may go on the wall of someone who wants to lie about shooting a trophy deer. Meat may be sold to specialty restaurants, and other items, both plant and animal parts may end up in a medicine shop in Thailand or China. There often is no scientific evidence for the effectiveness of these cures."

Wildlife officers have asked anyone witnessing one of these crimes to call 1-555-POACHER.

STUDENT HANDOUT 8

Session 7

Materials: Student Handouts 9–21, pages 37–49; Internet access for students during the second half of the session (optional)

Session Goal:
1. Continue to encourage students to utilize separate sources of data including maps and charts to develop a theory or come to a conclusion.

Procedures:
1. Have students sit with their group members.
2. Begin by giving students handouts 9–21 on pages 37–49.

What You'll See: Some groups may grasp the significance of older information and data as they are exposed to this new information. However other groups may merely glance at the maps and immediately ask, "Can we get on the Internet now?" Others who have at least learned that they are permitted to choose what they will do with their time simply may go to the computers and get online. In a sense this is good, because they are beginning to act like self-learners. Nevertheless, as a facilitator you may have to guide students to an understanding that today, time could be better spent reviewing and making connections about the data and information they already possess. During the second half of the session you may want to allow Internet access, but with the warning that they must be finding information elsewhere, and that Internet research will end at the next session.

What Could Go Wrong:
- Some students may be experiencing a level of frustration that is impeding progress. (In my experience, it happened at Session 8.) If that is the case, you may want to devote part of the class to lateral thinking techniques or activities. If you do not have activities of your own, you may want to use Handouts 23 and 24 (pp. 52–53) here, instead of during Session 8.
- If you used those activities during the last session, you may consider using one of the activities on Handouts 27 or 28 on pages 56 and 57. Do not do both. Students will need a mental break later on while developing theories, action plans, and presentations.

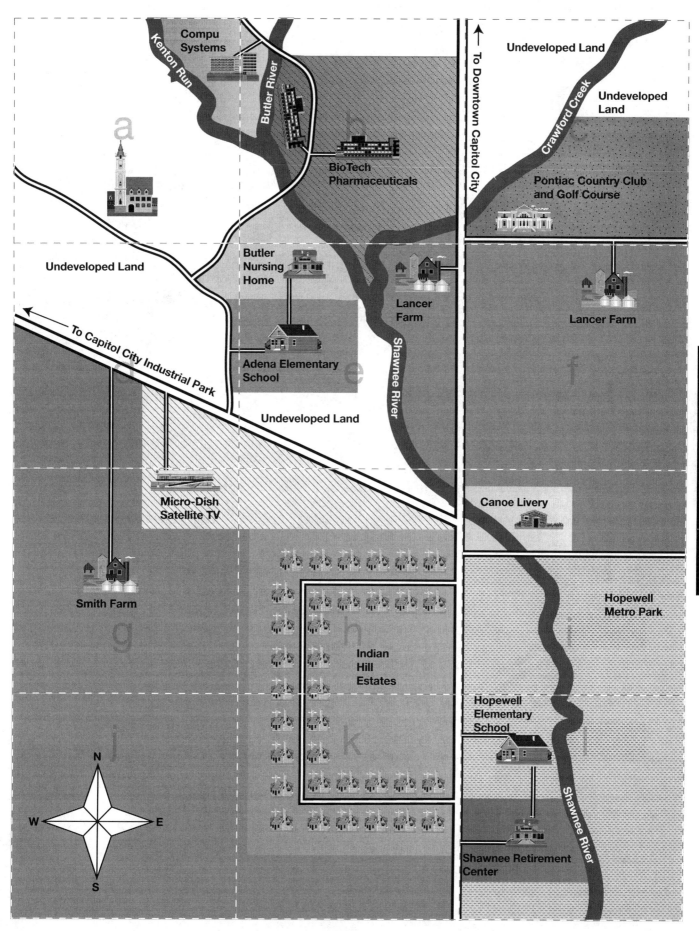

Compu Systems

Kenton Run

Butler River

a

BioTech Pharmaceuticals

Undeveloped Land

Undeveloped Land

Crawford Creek

To Downtown Capitol City

Pontiac Country Club and Golf Course

Undeveloped Land

Butler Nursing Home

b

Lancer Farm

Lancer Farm

f

Adena Elementary School

e

Shawnee River

To Capitol City Industrial Park

d

Undeveloped Land

Micro-Dish Satellite TV

Canoe Livery

Hopewell Metro Park

i

Smith Farm

g

Indian Hill Estates

h

Hopewell Elementary School

j

k

l

N
W E
S

Shawnee Retirement Center

Shawnee River

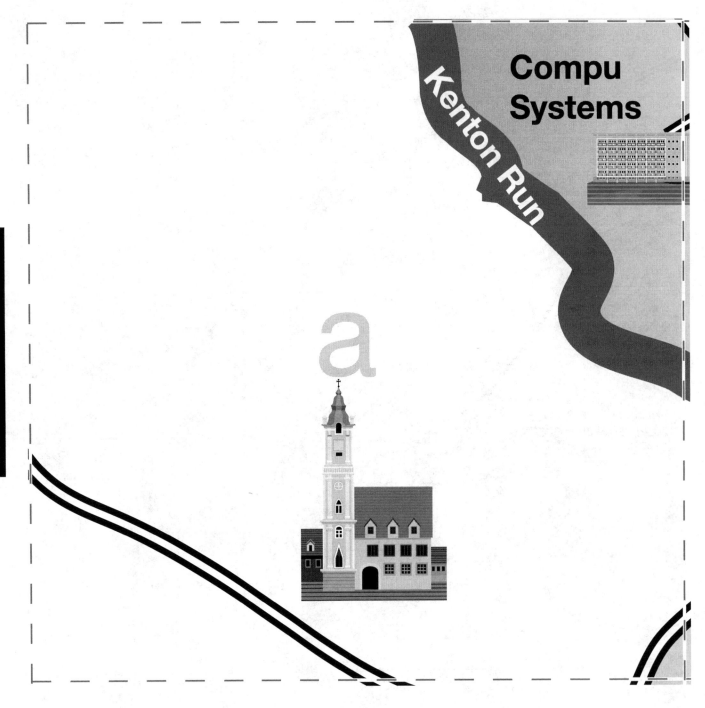

Compu
Systems

Kenton Run

a

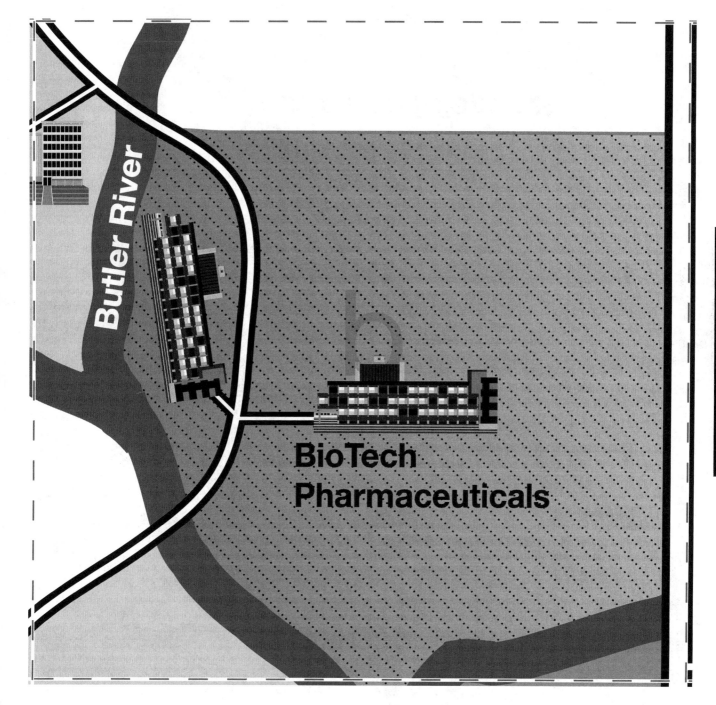

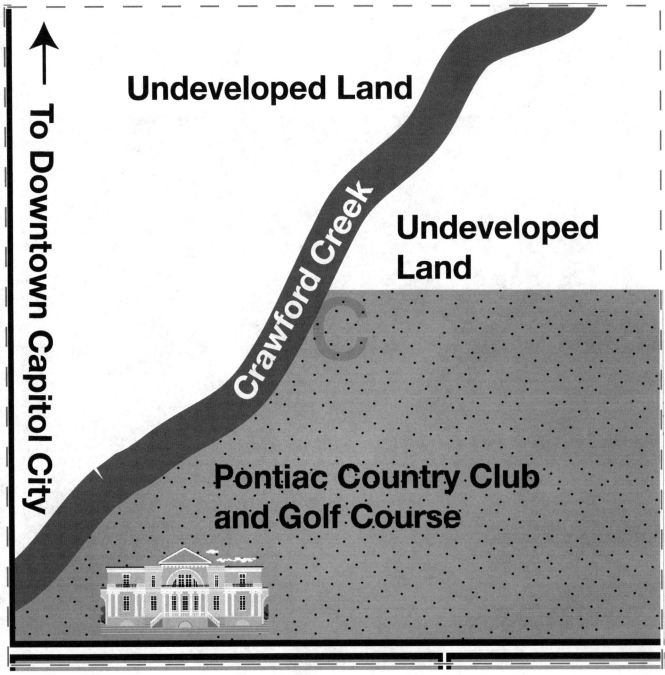

To Downtown Capitol City

Undeveloped Land

Crawford Creek

Undeveloped Land

Pontiac Country Club and Golf Course

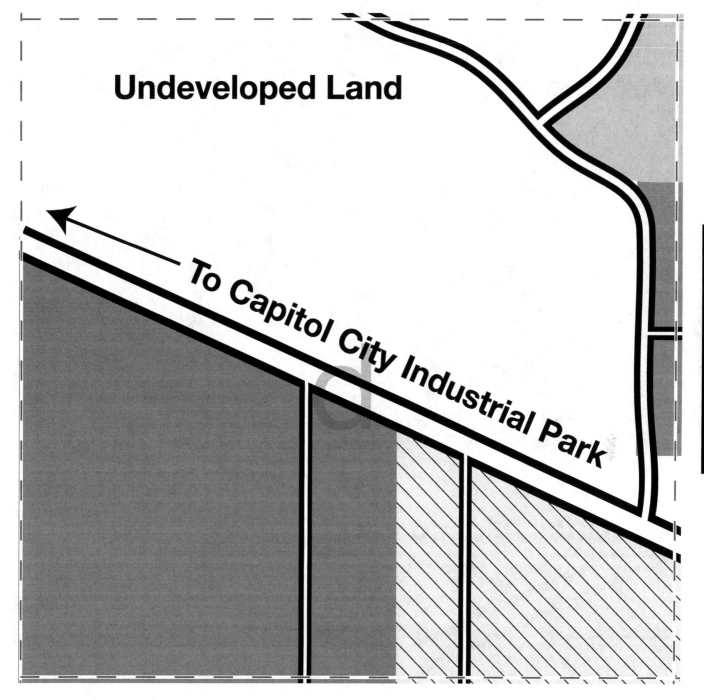

Undeveloped Land

To Capitol City Industrial Park

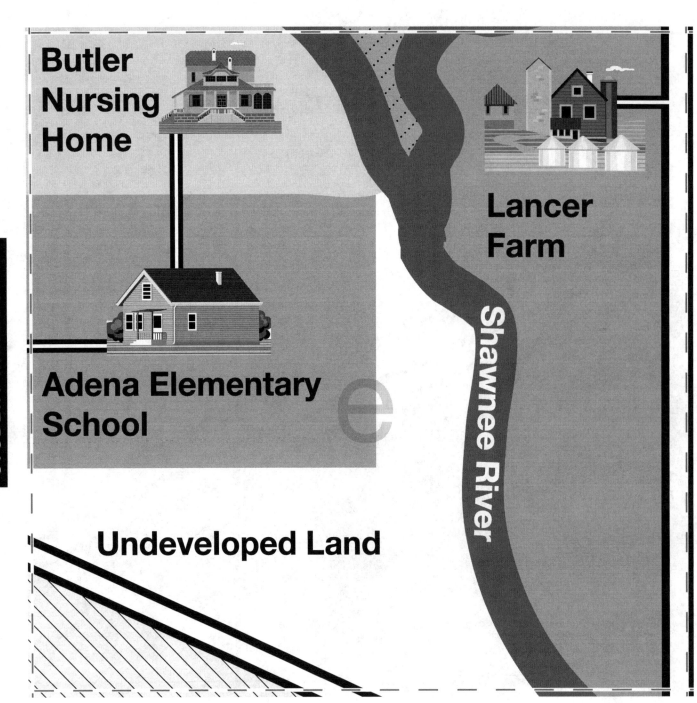

Butler Nursing Home

Lancer Farm

Adena Elementary School

Shawnee River

Undeveloped Land

Lancer Farm

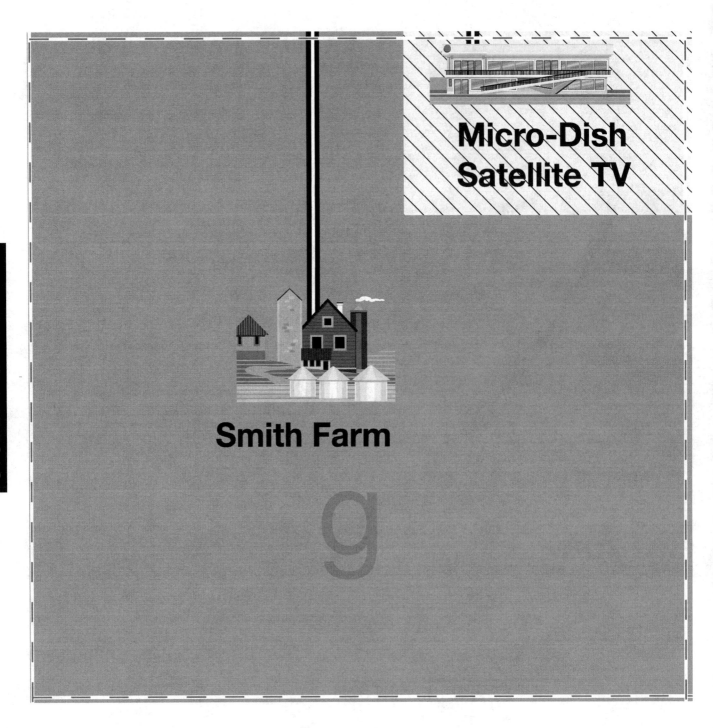

Micro-Dish
Satellite TV

Smith Farm

g

Indian Hill Estates

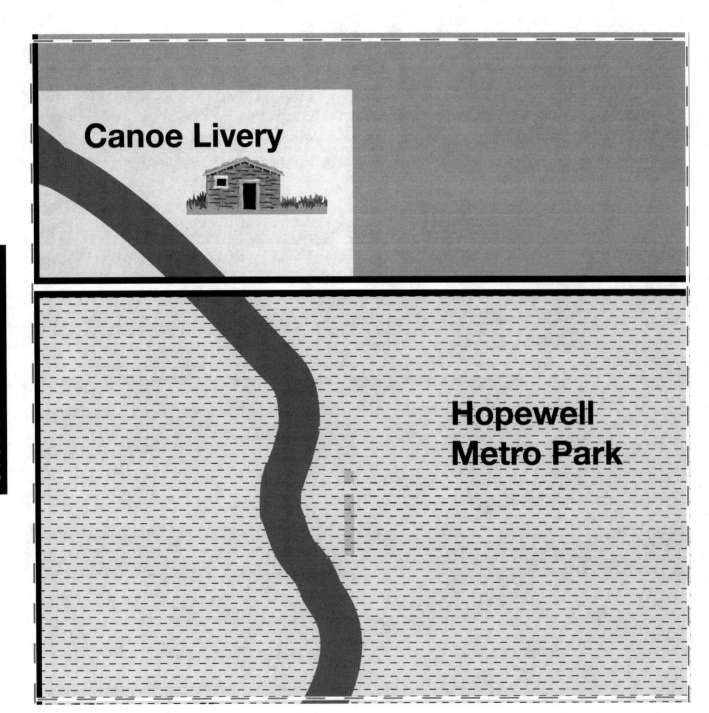

Canoe Livery

Hopewell
Metro Park

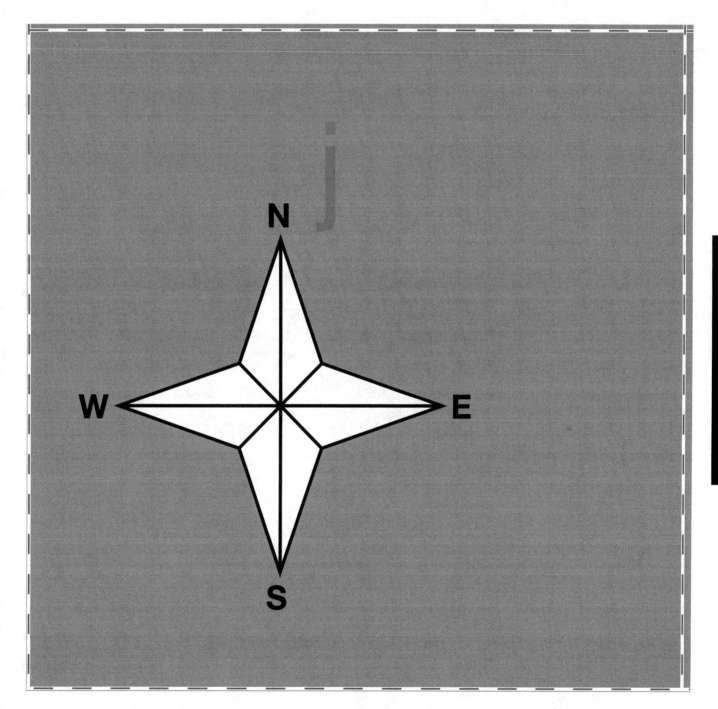

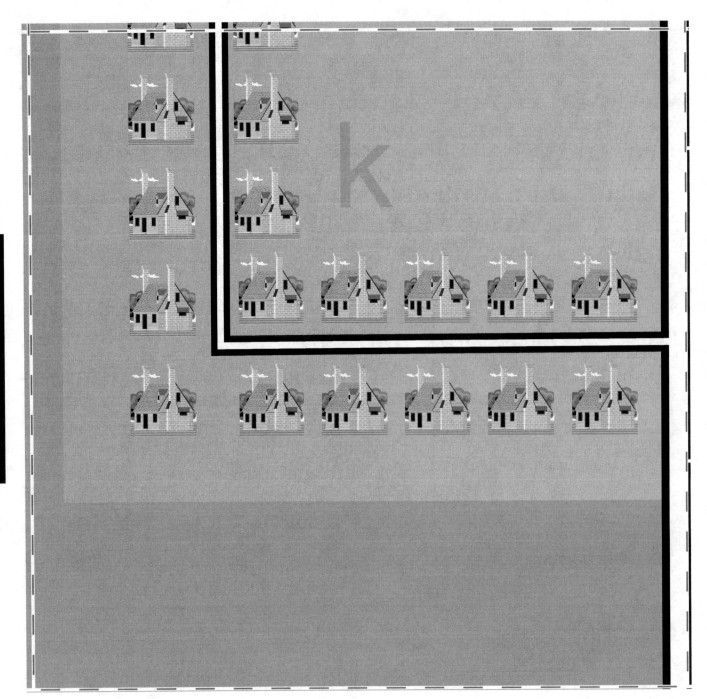

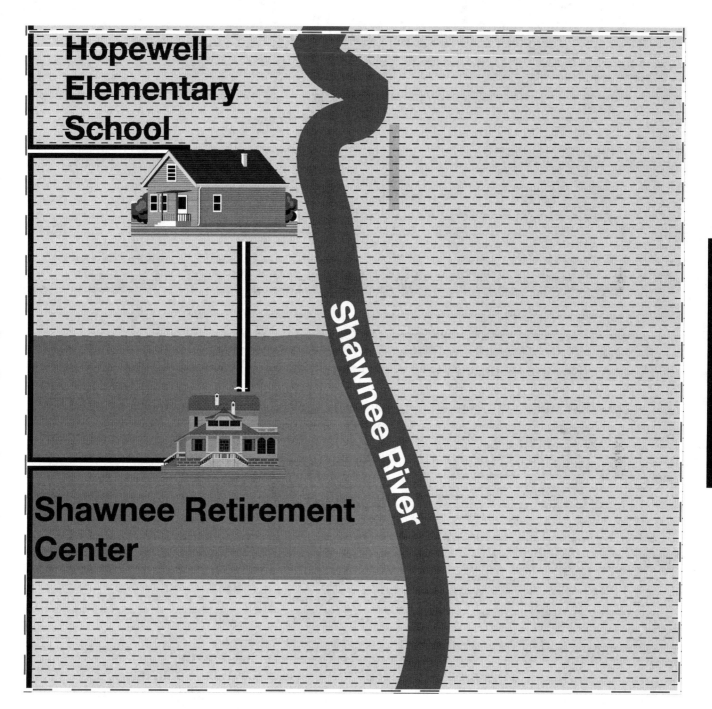

Session 8

Materials: Student Handouts 22–35, pages 51–64; Internet access for students during the second half of the session

Session Goals:
1. Continue to encourage students to utilize separate sources of data including maps and charts to develop a theory or come to a conclusion.
2. Help students begin to understand various types of progressions and patterns—both mathematical and nonmathematical.

Procedures:
1. Have students sit with their group/team members.
2. Have students read Handout 22.
3. Have students or student groups work through Handouts 23–25 one at a time. Include whole-group discussion of each handout before proceeding to the next one.
4. Discuss patterns and points of view. Ask (without giving away any group secrets), "How can what we have just done be applied to our problem?"
5. Give students Handouts 26–35. Remind them to apply the principals they have just discovered concerning different types of patterns.
6. Allow Internet use (as needed) for the last time.

What You'll See: By now most groups will understand that data on the charts will probably be related to previous information. If not, simple questioning may help them discover that concept. You should see groups beginning to make connections among all of the information and data. You should see groups beginning to develop more reasoned and supportable theories regarding the disappearance of the mussels.

What Could Go Wrong:
- Some students or groups may be failing to make connections. Your questioning with these students may need to be a bit more direct. You might need to ask, "How could we apply what we learned from Handouts 23–25 to the information we already have or to the new charts?"
- Caution: You do not want to ask specific yes or no questions or questions that reveal specific information or connections within this problem.

MEMO:
Date: October 21
From: Allen Stevens
To: The Shawnee River Mussel Investigation Committee
Re: Weekly Update

Thank you again for all of your help. Your hard work continues to be an inspiration to everyone in this community. I am particularly pleased with those of you who have been more concerned with asking questions, rather than jumping to early and unsupported conclusions.

I'm sure you will continue to uncover information that will be helpful. However, you should be aware that the next time we meet, I'll be expecting to hear your initial thoughts concerning what might be causing the mussels to be disappearing from the Shawnee River.

I have received wildlife sighting charts for the past 10 years from Mrs. Peterson. I will have them copied and I will get them to you later today. Mrs. Peterson reminded me that the charts were made by her fifth-grade students and are not necessarily a scientific study of the area wildlife. However, she feels the charts are a fairly accurate representation of what the students have seen from the classroom window and during their science walks in the schoolyard. When a student spots something he or she can identify, that student may add it to the chart. When other students see the same kind of animal, they may add a star to the chart. Once two stars are added, the sighting is "confirmed."

Please feel free to ask questions. If possible, I will provide your group with information regarding your question. That information may not be available to other groups working on the same problem.

Thank you again for your help. I'll look forward to talking with you soon.

You may contact me if you have any questions.

A. Stevens

Mr. Stevens
DSW Community Liaison

Progressions in Math

There are different kinds of progressions. We are most familiar with progressions that obey logical mathematical rules.

What are the next two numbers in each of the progressions below?

Explain the rule for the progression, using complete sentences. Some rules may take more than one complete sentence.

0, 2, 4, 6, 8, _10_, _12_

Starting with the number 0, add 2 to each number, to get the next number.

19, 17, 15, 13, _____, _____

4, 7, 10, 13, _____, _____

2, 4, 8, 16, _____, _____

0, 1, 4, 9, 16, _____, _____

0, 1, 1, 2, 3, 5, 8, _____, _____

Patterns

There also are progressions (patterns) in science and social studies. These patterns may be explained with numbers, but the rule may not be a mathematical rule. It may be a rule of science, nature, or of personal preference. In the example below, predict what will happen next. Explain the rule or reason for your prediction. Use complete sentences.

Mary at McDougal's

Mary went to McDougal's for lunch. She ordered a cheeseburger. The next time she went there she ordered a fish dinner. The next time she ordered a cheeseburger. The next time she also ordered a cheeseburger. The last time she went to McDougal's she ordered another cheeseburger.

If Mary goes to McDougal's for lunch today, what will she order? Explain your answer on the lines below. This question only requires a short answer. Please answer with two to three well-written sentences.

_____

_____

_____

_____

_____

© Prufrock Press Inc. • *Mystery River*

Cute Kittens

Mr. Davidson grew up in the Indian Hill area before it was part of Capitol City. "When I was a boy, we were way out in the country. My grandfather took me rabbit hunting across the river from Hopewell Elementary School. That was years before it became a park and hunting was no longer allowed."

Mr. Davidson and his family lived in Indian Hill Estates until a few years ago. Then they moved to a large farm about 15 miles farther south. "Now we're really out in the country. We have a barn where our children can have goats and a pony, and I can go rabbit hunting on my own property."

The first year Mr. Davidson harvested about 8 or 10 rabbits in his hunt. The children had just gotten their first goat and were in the barn feeding it when they saw three of the largest mice they could imagine. Mrs. Davidson is afraid of mice and wouldn't even go out to the barn after that, so Mr. Davidson brought three cats home one day and put them in the barn. Pretty soon the mouse problem was solved, and Mrs. Davidson even started going out to the barn again.

Everyone was excited when two of the cats had kittens. The children adopted the smallest one and kept it in the house, while the rest of the kittens grew up in the barn. The family never saw another mouse in the barn after that.

The next autumn Mr. Davidson went rabbit hunting again, but only saw one rabbit the whole hunting season. He was very upset.

What do you think Mr. Davidson will do next? This question requires an extended response. Please answer with a well-constructed paragraph of at least five sentences on the lines below.

_____

_____

_____

_____

_____

_____

_____

_____

_____

Fifth-Grade Animal and Large Bird Sightings 1999–2000

Picture	Animal Name	Confirmation #1	Confirmation #2
	Squirrel	✔	✔
	Minnow	✔	✔
	Mussel (Live)	✔	
	Otter	✔	✔
	Red Tail Hawk	✔	✔
	Snake	✔	✔
	Frog	✔	✔
	Muskrat	✔	✔
	Crayfish	✔	
	Rabbit	✔	✔
	Skunk	✔	
	Deer	✔	✔
	Blue Heron	✔	

Fifth-Grade Animal and Large Bird Sightings 2000–2001

Picture	Animal Name	Confirmation #1	Confirmation #2
	Squirrel	✔	✔
	Minnow	✔	✔
	Mussel (Live)		
	Blue Heron	✔	
	Muskrat	✔	✔
	Otter	✔	
	Red Tail Hawk	✔	✔
	Snake	✔	
	Frog	✔	✔
	Crayfish	✔	✔
	Rabbit	✔	✔
	Deer	✔	✔

Fifth-Grade Animal and Large Bird Sightings 2001–2002

Picture	Animal Name	Confirmation #1	Confirmation #2
	Squirrel	✔	✔
	Minnow	✔	✔
	Snake	✔	✔
	Crayfish	✔	✔
	Frog	✔	✔
	Skunk		
	Red Tail Hawk	✔	
	Rabbit	✔	✔
	Deer	✔	
	Duck	✔	✔
	Muskrat		

© Prufrock Press Inc. • *Mystery River*

Fifth-Grade Animal and Large Bird Sightings 2002–2003

Picture	Animal Name	Confirmation #1	Confirmation #2
	Minnow	✔	✔
	Squirrel	✔	✔
	Snake	✔	
	Crayfish	✔	
	Frog	✔	✔
	Deer	✔	✔
	Red Tail Hawk	✔	
	Rabbit	✔	✔
	Snow Owl		
	Duck	✔	✔
	Blue Heron	✔	✔
	Muskrat	✔	

Fifth-Grade Animal and Large Bird Sightings 2003–2004

Picture	Animal Name	Confirmation #1	Confirmation #2
	Minnow	✔	✔
	Squirrel	✔	✔
	Snake	✔	
	Crayfish	✔	
	Frog	✔	✔
	Deer	✔	✔
	Red Tail Hawk	✔	
	Rabbit	✔	✔
	Snow Owl	✔	✔
	Duck	✔	
	Blue Heron		
	Groundhog	✔	
	Fox		

STUDENT HANDOUT 30

Fifth-Grade Animal and Large Bird Sightings 2004–2005

Picture	Animal Name	Confirmation #1	Confirmation #2
	Minnow	✔	
	Mussel (Live)	✔	
	Squirrel	✔	✔
	Snake	✔	✔
	Crayfish	✔	✔
	Muskrat	✔	
	Duck	✔	✔
	Deer	✔	✔
	Red Tail Hawk	✔	
	Rabbit		
	Groundhog	✔	
	Coyote		
	Fox		

Fifth-Grade Animal and Large Bird Sightings 2005–2006

Picture	Animal Name	Confirmation #1	Confirmation #2
	Squirrel	✔	✔
	Mussel (Live)		
	Crayfish	✔	✔
	Snake	✔	
	Minnow	✔	✔
	Duck	✔	
	Deer		
	Red Tail Hawk	✔	✔
	Rabbit	✔	✔
	Groundhog	✔	
	Otter	✔	
	Muskrat	✔	✔

Fifth-Grade Animal and Large Bird Sightings 2006–2007

Picture	Animal Name	Confirmation #1	Confirmation #2
	Squirrel	✔	✔
	Mussel (Live)	✔	
	Crayfish	✔	✔
	Snake	✔	✔
	Minnow	✔	
	Duck	✔	
	Deer	✔	✔
	Red Tail Hawk		
	Raccoon	✔	
	Rabbit	✔	✔
	Groundhog	✔	✔
	Goose		
	Skunk	✔	
	Muskrat		

© Prufrock Press Inc. • *Mystery River*
This page may be photocopied or reproduced with permission for classroom use.

STUDENT HANDOUT 33

Fifth-Grade Animal and Large Bird Sightings 2007–2008

Picture	Animal Name	Confirmation #1	Confirmation #2
	Squirrel	✔	✔
	Minnow	✔	✔
	Crayfish	✔	
	Snake	✔	✔
	Duck		
	Deer	✔	✔
	Fox		
	Rabbit	✔	
	Groundhog	✔	✔
	Goose	✔	✔

STUDENT HANDOUT 34

Fifth-Grade Animal and Large Bird Sightings 2008–2009

STUDENT HANDOUT 35

Picture	Animal Name	Confirmation #1	Confirmation #2
	Squirrel	✔	✔
	Minnow	✔	✔
	Raccoon		
	Crayfish	✔	
	Snake	✔	✔
	Fox		
	Groundhog	✔	✔
	Deer	✔	✔
	Goose	✔	✔
	Coyote	✔	
	Frog		
	Otter	✔	

Materials: Student Handouts 36–38, on pages 67–69

Session Goals:
1. Break time! Today is a day to step back, relax, regroup, and take a break.
2. Give students Student Handout 36 for them to add to their files of information. After Student Handout 36, student will receive only one more piece of common information, which will come in the next session.
3. Groups may be experiencing data overload. You may see groups fumbling through stacks of handouts and printouts. They may have buried themselves in a pile of disorganized paper.
4. The activities on Student Handouts 37 and 38 are student favorites. If you have already used one of them use the other today and bring one of your own. They will help students relax while reinforcing lateral thinking skills that will be invaluable in the coming sessions.
5. Students also should use this day to organize their information and discard truly irrelevant materials.

Procedures:
1. Have students sit in a large circle—not as groups.
2. Work through the critical thinking activities on Student Handouts 37 and 38. Do not give students the answers. One way to facilitate these activities, without spoon-feeding answers, is to allow students to ask any question regarding the scenario, as long as the question can be answered with either "yes" or "no." If you must resume after lunch or after recess or even on another day, so be it, but do not give the answers. Require students to ask questions until they have succeeded.
3. After students have solved the problems on Handouts 37 and 38 (or after you feel you have devoted as much time to solving one or both of them as you should for the day), tell students that the rest of this session will be devoted to a review of what they already know, a reorganization of data and research findings, and a time to discard irrelevant papers and information.
4. Quietly approach each group (so other groups cannot "steal" ideas), and question them regarding their theories. Let them know ahead of time that you will be doing this, and that you will expect each group to share a minimum of two supportable theories.
5. At some point in this session (and again in the next two sessions), make a point of asking if, based on what they already know, there is anything else the group would like to know. See the Special Memo handouts in Appendix A on pages 88–90 for information that may be given to one or more groups, but not to others, based on group requests.

What You'll See: Students will appreciate a "fun day" and will approach the next phase of the unit with a renewed freshness and sense of organization and control.

What Could Go Wrong:

- As you begin your questioning, some students or groups may insist that there is only one right answer. They should be challenged to complete another knowledge tree activity (or several tree activities) each beginning with one or more of their ideas or pieces of information or data.

MEMO:

Date: October 23

From: Allen Stevens

To: The Shawnee River Mussel Investigation Committee

Re: Weekly Update

Thank you again for all of your help. Your hard work continues to be an inspiration to everyone in this community. I am pleased to see that many of you are focusing on the importance of asking questions.

Of course, at some point, we all must make connections among all of the things we have learned from our questioning. As you have been making those connections, I'm sure you have developed a plausible theory of what has happened to the mussels in the Shawnee River. There is only one week left until you are to make your presentation to the Department of Streams and Wildlife. Therefore, I will be talking with you later today, and I will expect you to be able to share your theory, along with *two or more* pieces of evidence to support that theory.

I'm sure you realize that knowing the problem is only the first step. Understanding the problem is not enough. We also must understand what (if anything) can be done to correct the problem. Nobody likes to hear that nothing can be done to fix a bad situation, so I also will expect you to begin to develop a plan of action to correct this problem. Remember, you only have a week to develop your plan of action, so you should be focusing your efforts on that plan and on your presentation.

A. Stevens

Mr. Stevens
DSW Community Liaison

Illuminate Your Mind
(It Makes Sense, If You Use Yours)

You are alone. No one will come to help you.

You are in the basement of a house with no way of seeing into the attic. In the basement are three light switches. Each switch turns one light bulb in the attic on and off. There is no way to trace the wires from a switch to its light bulb.

While in the basement, you may turn switches on and/or off in any order or in any way you want.

After leaving the basement to go to the attic, you may not return to the basement.

You go to the attic *one time*. Tell how (while in the attic) you can know *for sure* which switch in the basement is responsible for turning which light in the attic on and off.

To help you determine how this can be done, you may ask your teacher any question, as long as the question can be answered with either "yes" or "no."

Remember, every time you get an answer to one question, that answer should cause you to wonder about something else, and should help lead you to your next question.

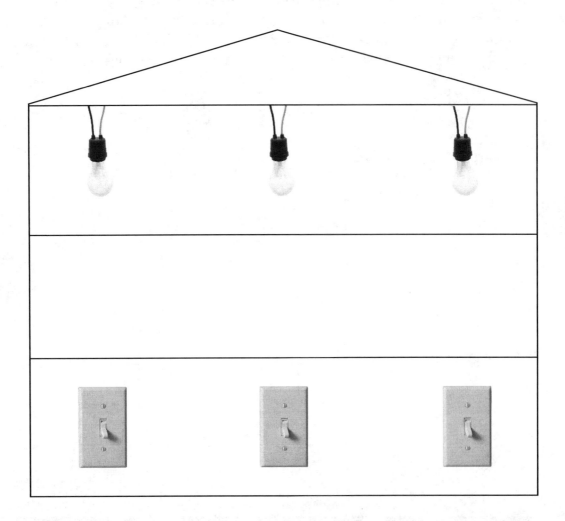

Camel Jockeys
(Words Mean Things)

Far away, in a land of sand, lived a wise and wealthy merchant. This merchant had made his fortune by working long and hard, guiding his camel caravans to lands even farther away. But alas, his two sons wanted to do nothing more than raise and race camels for fun. Each son bragged that his camel was the fastest in all the land.

The time came when the wise and wealthy merchant knew that his fortune would soon go to someone else. The custom of the land required that he give his entire fortune to only one of his sons; but to which one should he give it? He wanted to give his fortune not just to someone who could make his camel go fast, but to the one who really understood camels—to someone who could control any camel and eventually control an entire caravan and make his own fortune.

The father sent messages to his two sons, telling each to get his fastest camel and to come to his father. When the sons arrived at their father's tent, the father said, "My sons, the time has come for me to give everything I own to one of you. Because I can only give what I own to one of you, here is how I will decide between you. I see you have each brought your fastest camel. I want you to race the camels to the oasis that is 50 miles south of here, and back again. You must begin now, and you must keep your camels moving. You may only stop when you get to the oasis, and then you may rest and water your camels. However, you must begin the race back to my tent within one day of the time you arrive at the oasis. The one of you whose camel gets back here *last* will inherit everything I own."

The sons got on their camels, and began toward the oasis as slowly as possible. In fact, they walked the camels so slowly that both they and the camels almost died of thirst before they arrived. After watering their camels and drinking all of the water they wanted, the brothers sat down to rest and discuss their problem. If they did the same thing on the way home they would surely die. Yet, neither was willing to let his brother win the contest and inherit their father's fortune. They knew that the custom of the land would not allow the winning brother to share the fortune with the loser.

Just as it was about time to leave, they noticed (on the other side of the oasis) a very small tent of an old wise man. The brothers greeted the wise man respectfully and told him of their dilemma. They then humbly asked the wise man for his advice. The wise man thought for a moment and then gave them his advice.

Immediately the brothers ran to the camels, jumped on, and raced for home as fast as possible.

What advice did the wise old man give the brothers?

Session 10

Materials: Student Handout 39, on pages 72–73

Session Goals:

1. Continue to help students to understand that information or data that was previously deemed irrelevant may indeed have value in light of new material.
2. See students become willing to accept new information/data even if that information requires them to alter their own theory or plans.

Procedures:

1. Have students sit with their group members.
2. Begin by giving students Student Handout 39 on pages 72–73. Allow as much time as necessary for groups to assimilate the new information
3. At some point in this session (and again in the next session), make a point of asking if, based on what they already know, there is anything else the group would like to know. See the Special Memo pages (Appendix A; pp. 88–90) for information that may be given to one or more groups, but not to others, based on group requests. You also can copy the Confidential graphic on page 90 to give a sense of secrecy to the information that will encourage others to keep asking questions so they can see the secret information too.
4. Ask groups if they read anything in this newspaper they feel is significant. If not, you may become more direct in your questioning by asking whether anything in this newspaper conflicts with any of their previous information, data, assumptions, theories, or conclusions.

What You'll See: Some students or groups may see things falling together nicely—at least from their perspective. However, other groups may become a bit panicked if new information/data conflicts with their current understanding. You will want to be encouraging and supportive in either case; however, you cannot allow students or groups to ignore inconvenient information or data.

What Could Go Wrong:

- Students or groups may choose to ignore or gloss over inconvenient information or data.
- Differences in opinion between or among group members may begin to become an impediment to progress. You may need to spend some time at the beginning of this or one of the next one or two sessions helping students understand group decision-making processes (see the resources section of this book's introduction).

- If you have not already done so, you will want to confirm all aspects of the day of final presentations including the judges, the room availability, and invitations to parents and other relatives.
- Take note of materials the students need to supply for the next session.

Capitol City Dispatch

—October 23, Issue 24

EPA Sues Capitol City

EPA officials filed a lawsuit in federal district court last week, charging Capitol City with environmental safety code violations. Also charged in the lawsuit is EnviroMax, the city's out-of-state supplier of lawn care and landscaping services. EnviroMax maintains the grounds of all city-owned office property, the city parks, and the city's three public golf courses.

EnviroMax also provides chemical spraying for mosquito control during the time of year when mosquito populations are at their peak.

The suit charges the city and EnviroMax with using the pesticides in a manner not permitted by the labeling. EnviroMax also is charged with failing to adequately protect its employees while they were applying the

pesticides. The suit also alleges that EnviroMax applied more than the maximum amount of fertilizers and pesticides at the city-owned golf courses.

The city is charged with failing to adequately supervise a company providing services for the city, and with failing to provide adequate warning to citizens about the risks involved in the program, and with failing to adequately inform citizens when spraying would take place in their neighborhood.

The city's health department had requested the spraying to control disease-carrying mosquitoes and to reduce the risk of West Nile Virus. Last year, there were three confirmed cases of West Nile Virus in humans in

Capitol City. One woman died from the virus.

There were no reported cases of the virus in humans this year, and health department officials credit EnviroMax's aggressive spraying campaign with eliminating the disease and saving lives this year.

The mayor would only say that the city has done nothing wrong, and referred questions the city law director's office.

Owners of private golf courses in and around the city assured the Dispatch that the EPA suit does not involve them. Twin Pines Country Club manager Nelson Patterson said they use a reputable local lawn care company for their golf course.

Hazmat Called to Help Boy Scouts

Hazmat teams from Capitol City and two surrounding counties responded to a request for help from Boy Scout Troops 124 and 318 about 5:30 p.m. yesterday evening. The scout troops were conducting their monthly cleanup of a mile-long section of Kenton Run just south of Maple Lake Park, when they discovered a 40-gallon barrel that was leaking an unknown substance.

Hazmat teams arrived by 5:50 p.m. and secured the area. After applying an absorbing and drying agent to the area around the drum, the crew moved the drum and its remaining contents. Tests will be performed to determine the exact ingredients in the contents of the drum.

"It smelled awful and kind of burned your nose," said David Phillips of Scout Troop 318. None of the other scouts complained of adverse effects from coming in contact with the hazardous material. Nevertheless, city health officials were called to check each scout and adult leader.

"Other than the two scouts who initially found the drum, everyone stayed pretty far away," said Dr. Melissa Brownson, of the city health department. "They were careful and did the right thing."

Police detectives and crime scene investigators also were on the scene, collecting evidence and interviewing residents near the river. EPA officials are currently collecting water samples above and below the dumpsite on Kenton Run, as well as from selected points in the Butler River.

Villains Zapped at ComCon

In what reminded many of a Gotham City Swoop, or a Dick Tracy Take Down, the antipiracy joint task force comprised of state police, local undercover detectives, and Treasury Department agents descended on last weekend's comic book convention at the Capitol City Convention Center. Agents made 32 arrests and confiscated more than 10,000 illegal DVDs from 23 different vendors. Estimates on the street value of the pirated DVDs range from $15,000 to $23,000.

Many people attending the weekend ComCon event thought the raid was just part of the show, but the villainous vendors knew better, and are finding out that, just like in the comic books that surround them, crime doesn't pay.

Unfortunately, for some of these real-life pirates, the temptation to cash in on part of a multibillion-dollar illegal trade market each year is just too much to resist. For years, these thieves have tried to blend in with legitimate dealers at comic book and computer conventions, as well as flea markets throughout the country.

Undercover heroes, posing as legitimate vendors, have been a good source of information for the task force in Capitol City, and for other law enforcement officials across the country. The comic book convention continued without further incident.

Session 11

Materials: None from the teacher, unless appropriate special requests are made by groups (see the three memos entitled Special Memo on pages 88–90; these can be given to students with the proper requests). Students should bring any materials they need for creating charts, graphs, posters, brochures, or any other visual aids they plan to use in their final presentations.

Session Goal:

1. Students will review all of their information, finalize the development of their theories and action plans, and begin the development of their final presentations.

Procedure:

1. As groups meet, the job of teacher/facilitator is to lend support while avoiding any direct input.

What You'll See: As groups develop presentations, one tendency is for group members to each "take a part." You may hear things similar to, "I'll talk about the flooding and you talk about the pollution." Although there must be some division of roles and responsibilities, you should encourage everyone in the group to be familiar with all aspects of the group's theory and action plan. It is uncanny how a key group member (often the dissenter) can become ill on the day of presentations. As groups discuss presentation strategies, intragroup conflicts are all but inevitable. Your task is to mediate these disagreements and encourage students to use group decision-making and conflict resolution strategies to come to a consensus.

What Could Go Wrong:

- Other than total emotional meltdown by a high-intensity individual whose ideas are dismissed by the rest of the group (yes, it happened in one of my schools), there is not much to really go wrong at this point.
- Some students ask, "May I take the poster (or something else) home to work on there?" After several experiences of having a student forget to bring whatever was taken home back to school for the next session, I have evolved from replying, "Do you think that would be helpful?" to just saying, "No."

Session 12

Materials: None from the teacher, unless appropriate special requests are made by groups (then provide the three memos entitled Special Memo on pages 88–90). Students should be told that there will be no further information, even by request, after today. Students should bring any materials they need for creating charts, graphs, posters, brochures, or any other visual aids they plan to use in their final presentations.

Session Goal:

1. Students will review all of their information, finalize the development of their theories and action plans, and present the first draft of their final presentations.

Procedures:

1. As groups develop presentations, you will want to convey a sense of urgency. Students will be making the first oral presentation to you during the second half of this session. I have groups make presentations to me in the hallway, while other students are working in the room. This keeps other groups from stealing ideas. I sit by the door to watch other groups through the window.

2. Convey to your students that your role changes somewhat at this point. They need to understand that as they make their practice presentations to you, it is your job to make sure they are prepared to make their final presentations in front of professionals in the field they are studying and in front of parents and grandparents with a sense of confidence and competence.

3. During practice presentations, dispute their assumptions, question their data, challenge their logic, ask questions that you know they are not prepared to answer, and in short, become what some of my students have called "The Evil Judge." Students know this ahead of time. They know that no real judge will be this difficult. They also know you are merely playing a role and will, at some point, morph back into being their teacher, who will quietly ask them what they think they need to do to improve their presentation for the next time.

What You'll See: My experience is that initial presentations can be very poorly done. I have seen 3–5 students each taking a turn with their parts, and having the entire presentation last less than a minute! A quality presentation will last between 5 and 10 minutes, plus the time for judges' questions. Now is the time for whole-class, direct instruction regarding public speaking and presentation techniques (see resources section of this book's introduction).

What Could Go Wrong:

- The greatest danger now lies not with the students, but with the teacher. Do not underestimate the ability of students to recognize and correct their own weaknesses at this point.

Session 13

Materials: None from the teacher. Students should bring any materials they need for creating charts, graphs, posters, brochures, or any other visual aids they plan to use in their final presentations.

Session Goal:

1. Students will finalize the development of their final presentations and make those presentations to the teacher during the course of this session.

Procedures:

1. Give students a short time to work on their presentations.
2. Spend time in a whole-class activity, such as a readers' theater or other fun, public speaking, confidence-building activity.
3. Have the groups make their second presentation to you.
4. Discuss what it means to "dress professionally" for their final presentations.
5. Let students know that next week's "dress rehearsal" means that you will not comment, interrupt, or offer help during their presentation. It does not mean that girls need to wear dress clothes or that boys need to wear ties.

What You'll See: You will see a marked improvement both in the clarity of thinking and in the quality of presentations from practice to practice. This improvement should be enthusiastically noted and even celebrated, especially if you subscribe to "The Evil Judge" coaching model.

What Could Go Wrong:

*   Mr. or Miss Meltdown may still be the outsider. It happens. It is at this point that some of my students come to the realization that they will welcome the upcoming rigorous independent study I conduct each year. They just prefer working alone. Nevertheless, you must help that student understand that while a preference for solitude or complete control is OK, there are times that personal preference must be voluntarily set aside for the good of the group.
*   Final presentations happen just two sessions from now. Has another teacher scheduled a field trip, a written exam, or a party for the same time as your presentations? Do parents and others know the date, time, and place of the presentations? Has the local newspaper been contacted? Have judges been confirmed? Do they have copies of the information about the presentation, judges' sheets, and "The Right Answer" handout?
*   I still need to _____.

Session 14

Materials: None

Session Goal:

1. Students will make final dress rehearsal presentations to the teacher once (or twice at the group's discretion) during the course of this session.

Procedures:

1. Give groups a short time to gather materials and prepare mentally.
2. Have the groups make their first presentation of the session.
3. Remind students what it means to dress professionally for their final presentations.
4. Ask groups whether or not they want to make one final practice presentation.

What You'll See: You will continue seeing improvement both in the clarity of thinking and in the quality of presentations from practice to practice. Today is a day of praise and encouragement. Some groups still may not be presenting up to your expectations, but the time for anything other than praise and encouragement has passed.

What Could Go Wrong:

- Final presentations happen in the next session.
  Have you invited your principal?
- Do you have:
  - your still and/or video cameras ready?
  - new batteries?
  - film or extra media cards for cameras?
  - tape or disks for video cameras?
  - an assistant to photograph or videotape the presentations?
  - extra judging sheets?
  - confirmation of the room where presentations will take place?
  - arrangements for early access to the room for setup?
- I still need to _____ and
  _____.

Session 15

Materials: Copies of Note to Judges and Judges' Evaluation Sheet on pages 80–82

Session Goal:
1. Students will make final presentations for expert judges, family, and friends.

Procedures:
1. Arrive at least an hour earlier than usual to set up the room. If chairs and tables are movable, auditorium style seating works well, with a table in front for students, and one or more tables in the back for judges.
2. Set out judging sheets.
3. If the room size requires microphones, check the sound system.
4. Set up cameras.
5. Prepare any handouts for parents. This is a good time to promote your upcoming activities.

What You'll See: Nervousness. That is good. I often share with my students the anonymous quote, "If this situation doesn't scare you a little bit, then you are overconfident—and **that** should really scare you." The quote seems to help students understand that some nervousness is normal and even good. You'll also see pride and positive self-image after the presentations, both of which come from being challenged to do something that you didn't know you could do, and then doing it. (I, of course, knew that while the bar was set high, the task was achievable.)

What Could Go Wrong:
- Absolutely nothing! You have planned and prepared for this day. You've confirmed everything and double checked details. You are ready for this day. Enjoy it along with your students and their families.

Note to Judges

Dear _____

Thank you for taking valuable time from your schedule to meet with our students.

We hope to accomplish two things during the time you meet with them. In addition to having you evaluate the students' presentations, we would like you to share with our students information regarding opportunities that exist for a career in biology, wildlife management, outdoor education, or other related areas about which you are familiar.

In order to help you evaluate student presentations, I am enclosing a copy of all of the information that was given to students over the course of this unit of study. You may want to familiarize yourself with the general flow of the scenario. I also have included a page about "the right answer" to the problem.

I should emphasize the following:

- Students were only given the materials, information, and data I have enclosed here.

- Any other materials, information, or data the students had was obtained by them using their own efforts.

- There is not a right answer.

- Using only the materials, information, and data I have provided to the students, there is not one clear-cut cause for the disappearance of the mussels.

- Once a student group has developed a plausible and defensible theory of what caused the mussel disappearance, there may be several plausible and defensible courses of action that could be taken.

- The task of the students is to discover appropriate related knowledge and then to "make connections" among the information given to them and the knowledge they have discovered themselves. They are (from these connections) to develop a plausible and defensible theory, and suggest a reasonable course of action.

- The presentation of their theory and course of action should be done "professionally" and you may evaluate them based on the judging sheet provided.

- Because you are a professional, and have more knowledge and experience than our students, I would like you to ask questions of the students at the end of their presentations. For some students this may be their first public presentation. The answers to your questions may reveal as much or more about what they know than the "formal" part of their presentation. Please continue to ask questions until the group has exhausted its knowledge of the topic.

- However, please do not allow a particular personal bias or a particular area of personal knowledge or expertise to affect your judging. Your task is to evaluate their presentations for clarity, plausibility, and persuasiveness, and not to advocate for a particular scientific, social, or political position.

We will look forward to seeing you at _____ school, on

_____ at _____ a.m./p.m.

Thank you again,

Judges' Evaluation Form

Group #   1   2   3   4   5

Judge's Name _____

Note: As you rate criteria, 1 (or 2) is low and 10 (or 20) is high. A rating of 1 (or 2) equals 0% and a rating of 10 (or 20) equals 100%.
Please offer written comments. Use the back if necessary. Please rate the presentation on the following criteria:

1. Collection/Observation of Information/Data/Evidence
Meaning:
- Does the group show evidence of complete and accurate collection of information/data/evidence?
- Does the group show that they have collected information/data/evidence from sources other than what was given to them by the teacher?

    1   2   3   4   5   6   7   8   9   10

2. Logical Interpretation of Information/Data/Evidence
Meaning:
- Does the group make logical connections between and among pieces of information/data/evidence?
- Does the group make plausible and supported conclusions and suggestions?

    2   4   6   8   10   12   14   16   18   20

3. Presentation Skills
Meaning:
- Does the group make a professional presentation?
- Do they dress professionally? Can you hear the speakers? Do the speakers make significant eye contact with you? Do all group members contribute significantly to the presentation? Is the presentation made in a logical order? Are visual aids used? If so, are they appropriate?

    1   2   3   4   5   6   7   8   9   10

Evaluating and Debriefing

(This may be part of Session 15, or it may be considered a separate session.)

Materials: Learner/Facilitator Evaluation Form on pages 85 and 86; copies of the Judges' Evaluation Form; if available, video recordings of the presentations; if appropriate, student journals or thought logs.

Session Goals:
1. Students will reflect on their learning and group participation experience.
2. The facilitator also may provide a summative evaluation of student learning and group participation.
3. Students will develop an awareness and understanding of differing points of view.
4. Class will celebrate a job well done.

Procedures:
1. You know better than I do what is best for your students. You may choose to have students watch their own and each others' videos first, or you may think it better to have students immediately move to quiet areas for self-evaluation and/or journaling.
2. You may want to evaluate individuals at the same time, or not at all.
3. You may use the evaluation form provided, one you create yourself, or none at all, and only have students write about their experience.
4. In any case, self-reflection and self-understanding is critical to becoming a self-learner—a primary goal of this unit—so even though the excitement of the presentations may leave the students a bit on the active side, it is very important to get them quickly to the place where they can reflect and write.

What You'll See: You probably will see students who are very honest about their own performance and effort. Students often critique themselves more severely than the teacher does. You also will see more evidence of positive self-esteem from comments similar to, "I didn't think I could talk in front of the judges, but it was cool," or "I was scared at first, but when the judge asked me a question, I knew what to say and I think I surprised her." Some students may even say, "When I go to college, I think I want to study _____ and become a _____ like the judge."

What Could Go Wrong:
- Because you have probably already sent thank you notes to judges, your principal, and everybody else, there is nothing left to go wrong.

Learner/Facilitator Evaluation Form

Name _____

Keys:

1   I (or the student) exceeded the expectations of this category.

2   I (or the student) met most of the expectations of this category.

3   I (or the student) met some of the expectations of this category.

4   I (or the student) did not meet the expectations of this category.

W   I feel that I (or the student) did my (his or her) very best work in this category.

X   I feel that I (or the student) did very well, but not my (his or her) best in this category.

Y   I feel that I (or the student) did just enough work to get by in this category.

Z   I feel that I (or the student) did not put sufficient work into this category.

Please assign both a letter and a number to each of the following.

Personal Evaluation:

_____ _____ Use of time in class.

_____ _____ Use of time outside of class (at school and at home).

_____ _____ Individual contribution to the group project research.

_____ _____ Contribution to my group's final presentation.

_____ _____ Teamwork: Ability to lead or be led, as my group assignment dictated.

_____ _____ Attention to accuracy, completeness, and detail.

_____ _____ Attention to neatness.

Evaluation of Knowledge Gained From This Unit:

_____ _____ Knowledge of freshwater mussels.

_____ _____ Knowledge of the characteristics of high-quality stream water.

_____ _____ Knowledge of factors that may affect stream water quality.

_____ _____ Knowledge of how community values affect the decision-making process.

_____ _____ Knowledge, acquisition, and application of effective critical thinking skills.

_____ _____ Knowledge, acquisition, and application of effective group participation skills.

_____ _____ Knowledge, acquisition, and application of effective presentation skills.

Team Leaders Only:

_____ _____ My ability to organize and assign workloads.

_____ _____ My ability to accept suggestions from other team members.

_____ _____ My ability to keep our team working in a cooperative and friendly manner.

_____ _____ My ability to keep our team working on task.

_____ _____ Overall quality or level of excellence of my leadership skills.

Other Team Members Only:

_____ _____ My ability to accept my assigned workload.

_____ _____ My ability to see what needs to be done and offer constructive suggestions.

_____ _____ My ability to complete my assigned workload on time.

_____ _____ My ability to work as a cooperative and friendly team member.

_____ _____ Overall quality or level of excellence of my team participation skills.

My comments about this group learning experience:

_____

_____

_____

_____

_____

_____

_____

_____

Appendix A:
Special Memos

SPECIAL MEMO: BY REQUEST ONLY

From: Allen Stevens

To: The Shawnee River Mussel Investigation Committee

Re: Your Requested Information: Wastewater
        Treatment at Nursing Home and Retirement Center

Thank you again for asking specific relevant questions. Because you understand that asking questions is more important than making quick judgments, your group is receiving this information, which may not be available to other groups working on the same problem. Please treat this information confidentially.

Much of the Indian Hill area of Capitol City is not yet connected to the city's water and sewer system. Like most small to medium-size companies and organizations in this area, both Butler Nursing Home and Shawnee Retirement Center have their own wastewater treatment facilities. These facilities discharge into the Butler and Shawnee Rivers respectively. It may be noted that the same is true for Adena and Hopewell Elementary Schools.

We contacted officials from the State Environmental Protection Agency (EPA), who have monitored the water that is pumped from these four facilities into the rivers. EPA officials said they did not consider the purity of the water to be a problem. "Of course there are very small amounts of impurities in everyone's discharge water. That is true everywhere. Water in nature is never 100% pure water—not even the water you drink from the tap in your home. We at the EPA are concerned with the amount of impurities in the water, and whether or not they are dangerous."

Officials could not give us a specific list of impurities in the discharge water from the nursing home and retirement center, but they assured us that the "discharge water has always been within legal limits, both for types and amounts of impurities we test for." While not directly related to your specific request for information, you will be happy to know that EPA officials also confirmed BioTech's plan for hazardous waste removal, so that it does not enter the stream water.

Thank you again for your help. I look forward to talking with you soon.

You may contact me if you have any questions.

a Stevens

Mr. Stevens
DSW Community Liaison

SPECIAL MEMO: BY REQUEST ONLY
From: Allen Stevens
To: The Shawnee River Mussel Investigation Committee
Re: Your Requested Information: Possible Pollution by
        BioTech Pharmaceuticals

Thank you again for asking specific relevant questions. Because you understand that asking questions is more important than making quick judgments, your group is receiving this information, which may not be available to other groups working on the same problem. Please treat this information confidentially.

BioTech Pharmaceuticals (like most companies) creates unusable, and sometimes hazardous, byproducts during its manufacturing process. We contacted the public relations officer at BioTech, and she claims that all hazardous materials are transported (by truck) away from the area. We were told, "Hazardous materials are carefully taken to a federally approved dumping site in another state."

We also contacted officials from the State Environmental Protection Agency (EPA), who have monitored the water that is pumped from Biotech's manufacturing facility into Butler River. They noted that several years ago, there was a minor problem with the temperature of the water being discharged into the river. However, BioTech officials were cooperative and very responsive. EPA official Dr. Marvin Blackwell said, "A temperature problem often takes months to correct. BioTech solved its problem within a few weeks, and the temperature of the water discharged into Butler River has been within state and federal guidelines ever since then."

EPA officials said they did not consider the purity of the water to be a major problem, but did express concern about the amount of impurities found. "Of course there are very small amounts of impurities in everyone's discharge water. That is true everywhere. Water in nature is never 100% pure water—not even the water you drink from the tap in your home. We at the EPA are concerned with the amount of impurities in the water, and whether or not they are dangerous."

Officials could not give us a specific list of impurities in the discharge water from BioTech's factory, but they assured us that the "discharge water has always been within legal limits, both for types and amounts of impurities we test for." EPA officials also confirmed BioTech's plan for hazardous waste removal.

Thank you again for your help. I look forward to talking with you soon.

You may contact me if you have any questions.

A. Stevens

Mr. Stevens
DSW Community Liaison

This memo may be customized to meet your particular needs and/or to address questions from your students that are not covered in the included memos.

SPECIAL MEMO: BY REQUEST ONLY

From: Allen Stevens

To: The Shawnee River Mussel Investigation Committee

Re: Your Requested Information: _____

_____

_____

Thank you again for asking specific relevant questions. Because you understand that asking questions is more important than making quick judgments, your group is receiving this information, which may not be available to other groups working on the same problem. Please treat this information confidentially.

Thank you again for your help. I look forward to talking with you soon.

You may contact me if you have any questions.

A Stevens

Mr. Stevens

DSW Community Liaison

CONFIDENTIAL

Appendix B:
Tiered Vocabulary Activities
and Answer Key

Mystery River Vocabulary Word Search

```
C R R E N A T I L O P O R T E M S O H O
I N I M L T I M P L E M E N T N C K H H
Z O D E T A P R I T X E R W T O N S A R
F A C E T A U Q E D A N I A N N O C B O
H E R E D T A I L H A W K D A E B I E T
X I H A T L E R R I U Q S E V M D E W A
T M U S C L E N N E S M E N E O E N D T
R A O Q R Q E A Q Q G N U A L N R T O I
A A C X S A U L U D V L H O E E E I O L
C T C Q Z E L I E I E O F X R H G S F I
Q R S C I E R U R R P V T A N P N T R C
U R Q O O R N O C E X W E Z Y L A N A A
I I U I E O N I W O H I D L M E D M H F
R U I E S M N E M I N A U W O N N I M K
E Q R T E R L Q B R N I M Q R P E N R N
S S X N E L M U S S E L B A S E C M E U
W E T L W C O N S U L T W A R N U C D K
L B E B E U Q S E V I D E N C E B H X S
E T N T H W L A T N E M A D N U F X C K
C R A Y F I S H Z H B T C N I T X E I Z
```

Circle these words:

ADENA	EXTINCT	RACCOON
BINOCULARS	FOOD WEB	RED TAIL HAWK
CRAYFISH	MINNOW	SCIENTIST
DETERMINE	MUSCLE	SKUNK
ENDANGERED	MUSSEL	SQUIRREL

Word Search, continued

Circle the word that means or is:

The thing you are saying is actually about what is being discussed. (Starts with R)

Something that is an observable fact or event. (Starts with P)

Something that is related to, or characteristic of a large city. (Starts with M)

What you have is not enough, or the effort you are making is not sufficient to accomplish your goal.

You are going to put your plan into action.

Native Americans who came after the Adena, but lived in the same general geographic area.

That something is basic or of primary importance. (Starts with F)

Someone who helps you learn on your own.

A species has disappeared from a particular ecosystem. (Starts with E)

What you use to prove a point. (Ends with E)

Everything that surrounds and affects a living thing. (Ends with T)

To gradually create or produce something by deliberate effort over time. (Ends with P)

To ask someone for their advice or opinion.

To examine something in an effort to understand it—usually by looking at its parts. (Contains a Z)

To get or to obtain. (Contains a Q)

Mussel Crossword

Name: _____

Date: _____

© Prufrock Press Inc. • *Mystery River*

Mussel Crossword

Clues

ACROSS

1. Something that is of major significance or special interest
4. In Situation A of 44 Across, if half of the species that remain are endangered, how many species are endangered?
7. Used to watch wildlife from a distance
10. Not enough; not capable of
15. Everything that surrounds and affects a living thing
16. All insects have six legs. Lepidoptera are insects. Papilio glaucus is a Lepidoptera. Therefore Papilio glaucus _____
17. To decide
18. Factual information (as measurements or statistics) used as a basis for reasoning, discussion, or calculation
19. The quality or state of being likely to occur
20. Relating to or bearing upon the matter in hand
21. Although the species still exists in a few small areas, in most places it has been

    _____
23. To include with something else; to unite as one
24. Something that suggests proof
25. More than what is usual, proper, necessary, or normal
27. A person who does not teach very much, but still helps you learn much
31. May be obtained
33. To divide a complex whole into its parts
34. Arranging soil, rocks, or plant material for aesthetic or practical purposes
36. These are one of the larger water quality indicator species; they are crustaceans
39. Possibility; capable of development into actuality
40. To show, describe, or represent
41. Tissue in a body that causes movement when it contracts
42. A marine or freshwater bivalve mollusk
44. In Situation A, 5 out of 25 species of a particular animal have become extinct. What percentage has become extinct?

DOWN

2. A plan is of no value until you _____ it, or put it into action
3. Having to do with
5. The mathematical science of collecting, analyzing, and presenting data
6. A species threatened with extinction
8. Not false or imitation
9. Of central importance
11. After recent flooding and erosion, some species living in river bottoms may experienced stress or death due to _____
12. Of or relating to heavy manufacturing
13. An interval of time during which a sequence of a recurring succession of events is completed
14. In Situation A in 44 Across, what percentage remain?
19. An observable fact or event
22. Of, relating to, or characteristic of a large city
26. One place where students meet to study
28. One who maintains open lines of communication between two other people or groups
29. To ask the advice or opinion of
30. Remembered
32. No longer existing
33. To get or to obtain
35. To create or produce, especially by deliberate effort over time
37. These Native Americas antedated the Hopewell, but lived in the same general geographic region
38. All of the interacting chains of things eating and being eaten in an ecological community
43. A place that feeds, stables, and cares for horses for money, or that provides boats for rent

Thinking About Your Vocabulary

You have been abducted by aliens and taken to their Mothership. In order to be returned to Earth, you must convince the aliens that you can persuade other Earthlings to do whatever it takes to make sure endangered mussels do not become extinct. Before the aliens will return you to earth you must pass at least one, and possibly two or three tasks. Even if you are successful in the task or tasks and are returned to Earth, the aliens will erase three words from your brain. The aliens will give you a list of words and let you choose which three will be erased from your brain.

The aliens know that the following nine words are usually considered important when persuading people to save an endangered species:

Environment, Evidence, Extinct, Extirpated, Endangered, Scientist, Statistics, Probability, Research

In order to convince the aliens you are worthy of being returned to Earth, you must prove to them that, even if they erase three of those nine words from your brain, you can still persuade earthlings to save endangered mussels from extinction. Please understand that when the aliens erase a word from your brain, they also erase the concept of that word. So, if they erase the word *wolf* from someone's brain, they also erase wolves, wolf-like, wolfe, wolf-dog, Canis lupis, wolfen, "like a wild German Shepherd," and other related words, phrases, and concepts in all languages.

First: Choose which three words you are willing to have erased from your brain. Then, complete one of the tasks below.

Task 1. Give a reason (at least two complete sentences for each word) explaining how those words could be erased from your brain, without spoiling your ability to persuade other earthlings to save endangered mussels. Task 1 is mandatory. Your will be told which, if any, of the other tasks you must complete.

Task 2. Give a reason (at least two complete sentences for each word) explaining why the six remaining words are absolutely necessary to persuade other earthlings to save endangered mussels.

Task 3. Write a letter to your local newspaper, containing at least five well-written paragraphs, to persuade readers to become actively involved in making sure endangered mussels do not become extinct. You may not, of course, use the three words or related concepts that you will allow the aliens to erase from your brain. Also, you may not refer to the aliens in your letter.

Finally, compare your task or tasks with those of your classmates. Discuss similarities and differences among the words chosen, reasons given, and (if you completed Task 3) the way you tried to persuade others.

Answer Key

Student Handout 3

Information previously given indicates that each student usually makes a minimum of two necklaces. Students should use this and the information given on this handout to deduce the following:

2 classes × 25 students per class × 3 shells per necklace × 2 necklaces each = 300 shells needed

Students should be able to show and explain their work.

Student Handout 23

11, 9
16, 19
32, 64
25, 36
13, 21 (this last pattern includes the Fibonacci Numbers)

Student Handout 24

Defensible answers include cheeseburger, fish sandwich, or any other menu item. There is not enough data to make a solid conclusion. Students should provide at least two complete sentences stating an "answer" with a plausible reason for their answer.

Student Handout 25

Although this question presents many possibilities, there is not one clear answer. Students should provide at least three or four complete sentences stating an "answer" with a plausible reason for the answers.

Student Handout 37

Before allowing any questions, you should ask if any of the students are familiar with the story/answer. If so, they must say so and decline to participate, or be allowed to help you answer yes or no to the other students' questions. Here is the solution:

1. Flip switches A and B to the "on" position. Leave switch C off.
2. Wait for one minute.
3. Turn switch B to the "off" position.
4. Go quickly to the attic.
5. Light bulb A will be on, B will be off, but warm, and C will be off and cold.

Students also can get a similar answer by turning off switch A instead of B, leaving B the one that is still on in the attic. It often takes students a while to discard their assumption that you can only tell whether a light bulb is or has been on by looking at it. As students work through the *Mystery River* problem, they must be willing to approach data with both an open mind and a willingness to look at that data in unconventional ways.

Student Handout 38

The wise old man's advice was, "Switch camels and get back to your father's tent as quickly as possible."

Explanation: Words mean things. The father did not say that the son who gets back last wins, but that the one whose *camel* gets back last wins. By switching camels a son could win by getting back first on his brother's camel, thereby making his own (the one he owns) get back last. From the father's point of view, the son who could best control a camel he was not used to riding would be the best one to inherit his fortune.

As students work through the *Mystery River* problem, they must be willing to approach data critically and precisely.

Word Search

Mystery Words:

relevant
phenomenon
metropolitan
inadequate
implement
Hopewell
fundamental
facilitator
extirpated
evidence
environment
develop
consult
analyze
acquire

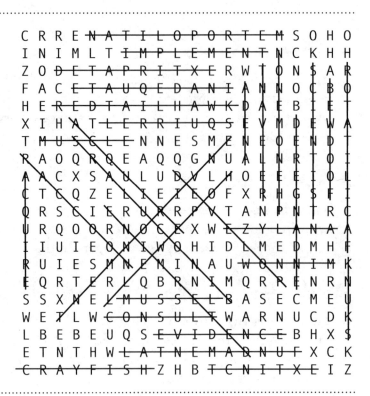

Mussel Crossword

Across

1. highlight
4. ten
7. binoculars
10. inadequate
15. environment

16. has six legs
17. determine
18. data
19. probability
20. relevant
21. extirpated
23. incorporate
24. evidence
25. excessive
27. facilitator
31. available
33. analyze
34. landscaping
36. crayfish
39. potential
40. depict
41. muscle
42. mussel
44. twenty

Down

2. implement
3. regarding
5. statistics
6. endangered
8. authentic
9. fundamental
11. siltation
12. industrial
13. cycle
14. eighty
19. phenomenon
22. metropolitan
26. classroom
28. liaison
29. consult
30. recalled
32. extinct
33. acquire
35. develop
37. Adena
38. food web
43. livery

The "Right" Answer

What Really Happened to the Mussels in the Shawnee River?

Problem-based learning by definition deals with situations that lend themselves to the possibility of more than one plausible theory/solution regarding the cause of the problem. PBL also assumes that for every plausible cause, there is more than one plausible course of action to correct/solve the problem. Judges should be encouraged to evaluate student presentations on the plausibility of the group's solution and course of action. They should be cautioned against judging groups based on a fixed answer to a similar problem in a particular locality. Judges also should be cautioned to avoid making judgments based on personal research or the latest article they just read in a professional journal, to which students do not likely have access.

Teachers equally may encourage groups whose theories and/or courses of action are very different from one another. However, as students work through the problem, it may be helpful for you to understand some of the clues that are built into the unit, in order for you to keep students from becoming overcommitted to a theory that will ultimately prove frustrating. The following information is for your use, and is not to be copied or given to students. With that in mind:

- The mussel population has been declining for several years. Although it only has been noted recently, it is not a sudden problem.
- This unit deals exclusively with freshwater (not marine/saltwater) mussels.
- There never will be a chemical analysis report available to students prior to the time they will be making presentations.
- Local businesses are indeed community minded. No business would intentionally do anything to harm the mussels, nor would it any "cover up" a known problem.
- Local farmers employ current best practices with regard to soil conservation. Although prehistoric increased maize production may have been associated with a decline of mussels, an increase in corn production itself is not associated with a decrease in mussels. There may, however, be unintended consequences of an increase in some agricultural activities that could affect mussels.
- Although there was significant flooding last spring, siltation from that particular flood could not have affected mussel populations during the preceding years.
- In some states (not all), mussel poaching is a concern. Deer poaching is much more common, and may or may not suggest mussel poaching.
- Municipal and privately owned sewage treatment plants are good at doing what they were designed to do. However, at the time of the writing of this book, there was no widespread use of a system designed to remove pharmaceuticals from wastewater.

- The EPA does not necessarily test for everything that could be in water.

I have been repeatedly asked what "really" caused the decline in mussel population. Fortunately, I have never shared an answer to that question with anyone. Sooner or later, word would get out and some enterprising fourth grader would just "look up the answer" on the Internet. What fun would that be?

I would, however, love to hear what your students think. I also collect videotapes of outstanding student presentations, so if you have one, along with the appropriate releases from parents, I would love to have a copy to share at professional development workshops. I also am available to facilitate workshops addressing problem-based learning and differentiated instruction for all students at your school, educational conference, or convention. You can contact me at:

Mark Bohland, M.Ed., M.Photog.
7250 Steam Corners Road
Lexington, OH 44904
419-884-1693
800-669-8512

Mark@ImproveAchievement.org
http://www.ImproveAchievement.org

About the Author

Mark Bohland is an educator, artist, and consultant. He is a graduate of Cedarville College and Ashland University, both in Ohio. He holds both Master of Education and Master of Photography degrees, and also is the author of *Mystery Disease*, published by Prufrock Press.

Mark began his teaching career in 1974. He has taught in both public and private schools, as well as inside the old, castle-like Ohio State Reformatory (where *Shawshank Redemption* was filmed). For the past 9 years, he has worked with academically gifted students in five different buildings per week, across two school districts, and two counties.

Mark's enthusiasm and dedication in the classroom have earned him a "Teacher of the Year" award from the Ohio Association for Gifted Children. His motivation and inspiration of students has been recognized with a Crawford County "Business–Education–Student–Teacher" award.

Mark and his wife Deborah live on a 3-acre mini-farm in rural North Central Ohio. There, they enjoy remodeling their more than 100-year-old farmhouse. Deborah restores long-neglected flower gardens and creates new ones, while Mark tries to reclaim old fruit trees and develop areas of native wildflowers, grasses, and other plants to attract butterflies and hummingbirds.

Mark has spoken to hundreds of teachers and artists at local, state, and regional conferences. An expert in differentiated instruction, Mark is available to facilitate workshops and provide in-class modeling, throughout the United States, Canada, and elsewhere.